Heart to Heart

Fourteen Gatherings for Reflection and Sharing

Christine Robinson and Alicia Hawkins

SKINNER HOUSE BOOKS
BOSTON

Printed in the United States

Text design by Suzanne Morgan / Cover design by Kathryn Sky-Peck
Cover art *Coda 4*, © 2007 Tracey Adams, www.traceyadamsart.com/

ISBN 1-55896-550-5 / 978-1-55896-550-8
6 5 4 3 2 1 / 13 12 11 10 09

Library of Congress Cataloging-in-Publication Data

Robinson, Christine C.
  Heart to heart : fourteen gatherings for reflection and sharing / Christine C. Robinson and Alicia Hawkins.
      p. cm.
  ISBN-13: 978-1-55896-550-8 (pbk. : alk. paper)
  ISBN-10: 1-55896-550-5 (pbk. : alk. paper) 1. Church group work. 2. Church group work—Unitarian Universalist Association. 3. Christian life—Study and teaching. 4. Christian life—Unitarian authors. I. Hawkins, Alicia. II. Title.
  BV652.2.R63 2009
  253'.7—dc22
                                                                                        2008046860

We gratefully acknowledge permission to reprint the following: Bible passages from the New Revised Standard Version (all unless otherwise noted), copyright 1989, Division of Christian Education of the National Council of the Churches of Christ in the United States of America, used by permission, all rights reserved; excerpt from *The Invitation by Oriah*, copyright © 1999 by Oriah Mountain Dreamer, and "It's possible I am pushing . . ." from *Selected Poems of Rainer Maria Rilke, A Translation from the German and Commentary* by Robert Bly, and "The tao that can be told . . ." from *Tao Te Ching by Lao Tzu, A New English Version, with Foreword and Notes*, by Stephen Mitchell, translation copyright © 1988 by Stephen Mitchell, and "Loose the cords of mistakes…" from *Prayers of the Cosmos: Meditations on the Aramaic Words of Jesus* by Neil Douglas-Klotz, copyright © 1990 by Neil Douglas-Klotz, reprinted by permission of HarperCollins Publishers; "The Guest House" by Mewlana Jalaluddin Rumi, translated by Coleman Barks, from *The Essential Rumi*, reprinted by permission of Coleman Barks; "Our Quiet Time" by Nancy Wood, from *Hollering Sun*, Simon & Schuster, 1972, used by permission of Nancy Wood; "I Am Not" by Juan Ramón Jiménez, translated by Robert Bly, from *Lorca and Jiménez*, Beacon Press, 1973, reprinted by permission of Robert Bly; "We Remember Them" by Sylvan Kamens and Jack Riemer, reprinted by permission; excerpt from "Funeral Blues," copyright 1940 and renewed 1968 by W.H. Auden, from *Collected Poems* by W.H. Auden, used by permission of Random House, Inc.; "Thank You for Your Loving Hands," from *Same Old Slippers* © 2008 Honey Pie Music, music © 1982 Judy Fjell, lyrics © 2000 Lisa Bregger and Judy Fjell, reprinted with permission; excerpt from "Take Something Like a Star," from *The Poetry of Robert Frost*, edited by Edward Connery Lathem, copyright 1949, 1969 by Henry Holt and Company, copyright 1977 by Lesley Frost Ballantine, reprinted by permission of Henry Holt and Company, LLC; excerpt from *The Prophet* by Kahlil Gibran, copyright 1923 by Kahlil Gibran and renewed 1951 by Administrators C.T.A. of Kahlil Gibran Estate and Mary G. Gibran, used by permission of Alfred A. Knopf, a division of Random House, Inc.; "When the animals come to us…" by Gary Lawless, from *First Sight of Land*, Blackberry Books, 617 East Neck Rd., Nobleboro, ME 04555, reprinted by permission.

Contents

Acknowledgments

This book was written with the help and support of many people, foremost our husbands, William Baker and Charlie Hawkins. Many of the participants in Covenant Groups at First Unitarian in Albuquerque helped to field test these readings, exercises, and format, and they kept that program going smoothly while we focused on writing this book. In addition, now that we understand fully what writing a book is like, we are especially grateful for our partnership.

Introduction

Exhausted from the chores of caring for an ailing family member, a woman dragged herself to her women's group one evening. She had not had time to do the reading, and she wondered if she would have the energy to listen to others share. But she was in charge of refreshments, so she went.

As the group gathered, she felt herself beginning to relax. Checking in felt like taking the invisible burdens off her shoulders and putting them down on the floor. She stumbled through her sharing, feeling incoherent and emotional. "This thing with my parents has been hard," she said, "but it's also been real. I'm not quite ready to say I'm glad it happened, but there have been some good things for my family and for me."

One woman in the group especially related to her sharing and remembered her own similar experiences and learning. Their eyes met in that moment, and they both understood that they were not alone. Although they had said no direct words to each other all evening, they had received strength and wisdom from each other. Two wild, shy hearts had met and been encouraged.

Something like that happened to us, and we thought it was important enough to design a structure where it would happen more often in groups created for sharing and growth. We realized that most people are unpracticed at deep sharing and supportive listening. We also realized that support groups and discussion groups often don't fulfill their potential of being safe places for deep sharing. Some people dominate; others feel they can't get a word in. Some people don't think well off the top of their head, and others chatter away but can't figure out how to share what is in their hearts. And while lots of people would like to be in these kinds of groups, it's hard to find someone willing to be a leader. We wanted to design a process that would make it easier to form sharing groups and more likely that they would work well. We wanted participants to share deeply and listen with open hearts to the wisdom of others, and we wanted the leader to have the same rich experience that participants did.

To meet these goals, we created a program called "Covenant Groups" at First Unitarian in Albuquerque. About five hundred people have participated over the years. We designed the group gatherings so that they would be manageable for the overscheduled people of our church and easy to lead.

The participants in our first year's groups told us over and over that they had never before had the opportunity to talk about their thoughts and feelings on deeply personal subjects or to hear others share heart to heart. They told us that the experience of feeling truly listened to was so close to feeling loved that they could hardly tell the difference. They told us that when they took what they had learned about listening into other parts of their lives, their lives were better. They were so enthusiastic about what they experienced that many signed up for a second and third year, became group leaders, and even began to write their own materials. The quality of careful, uninterrupted listening that they so valued started to seep into other parts of the congregation's life. Supper groups became more thoughtful, more people came home from church meetings feeling they'd been heard, and the silence in the sanctuary deepened.

The heart-to-heart group format offered in this book has now had five years of development in year-long, half-year, and three-gathering groups. For this book we chose the fourteen topics that generated the most meaningful discussions in the groups we've led. These were the conversations that took groups to a new level of connection and spiritual growth. This book has a companion website, www.HeartToHeartBook.com, which offers more resources and an additional gathering.

How to Form a Heart-to-Heart Group

Your religious community is an obvious place to look for people who want to join a heart-to-heart group, but support groups, neighbors, women's groups, or parents from your children's school are all groups that might like to try this kind of sharing. Six to eight people is an ideal size, but even two can do this work together. Couples or groups of friends can use these gatherings to deepen their relationship. It's not necessary to use every gathering provided in this book. We've had great success at First Unitarian introducing new members to the covenant group program in three-gathering "mini covenant groups." You can use these materials to foster conversation at family reunions, staff retreats, and similar gatherings, perhaps choosing just one subject and sharing time as a part of a longer program. We encourage your creativity!

Choose a place to meet, a time, and a schedule of gatherings. Ideally, groups meet twice a month, but once a month can work; so can a weekend retreat that includes four or five gatherings. Most gatherings will run around one hour and forty-five minutes; most groups plan on two hours to give some leeway. Other than the first and last gatherings, your group can address the topics in this book in any order. Some groups will meet in living rooms or congregational meeting rooms. If you can find a place where you don't have to meet around a rectangular conference table, you'll be more comfortable, but you will need some kind of small table, like a coffee table in the center of your circle.

If it is just not possible to form a group, you can use these activities by yourself, probably doing your sharing with your journal. Allow at least two weeks for each topic, returning to the activities, essay, and quotations several times. Try to pay special attention to what happens about the topic in the rest of your life during those two weeks.

Leadership

Once your group becomes accustomed to the gathering format, you may want to take turns leading. Sharing the leader's role can help the group mature, since everyone has an equal stake in the group. Even if you rotate leadership, there should be one leader who oversees the overall program and attends to any problems that may come up for the group.

At the end of this book (beginning on page 129), you'll find notes for leaders on each gathering—including what to think about in advance, what to bring, and how to manage tricky issues. It's important to consult these notes before leading a gathering.

Preparation

This book includes quotations, an essay, and activities to help you prepare emotionally and spiritually for each gathering. While we know how busy everyone is, we hope that at most gatherings, most group members will have done the preparation. The aim of this work is to get you thinking about the topic in advance so that you will come to the group more ready to share and more able to relate to what others are sharing. We hope that a little preparation will foster depth.

For each gathering, we offer several activities to give you choices in how much and what kind of preparation to do. You are encouraged to do as many activities and questions as you feel comfortable with and those that especially speak to you.

Many of the preparation activities involve writing or drawing. Find a journal that suits your personal style. Some people are content with a dime-store notebook; others prefer to purchase a pretty blank book with nice paper.

At the end of each list of activities is a paragraph that tells you what, if anything, to bring to the gathering and what you should be prepared to share. Keep time in mind as you plan your sharing, so that you can help the group stay within the intended time frame for the gathering.

Try not to put off your preparation until the last minute. Early preparation gives you time to think about how you feel and what you want to say. Of course, there will be times when you've just not been able to prepare. Go to your group meeting anyway!

The Gatherings

When you get to your first gathering, you'll discover that the sharing has a very firm structure, without the conversational back and forth you're used to. We think you will find, as many have before you, that this firm structure fosters a sense of safety and fairness in your group. It also frees the group leader from the chores of conversational traffic cop.

Each gathering follows a consistent pattern that includes the following elements.

Candle Lighting. The gathering begins with a short reading as a member of the group lights the candle.

On Our Hearts. Some weeks you will come to the group with wonderful news or a heavy heart, and it will be important for the group to know what's going on with you. A few minutes are set aside for this kind of sharing. In addition, the leader will let you know about any absent members at this time. This is not meant to be a check-in, where each group member talks about his or her week. It is really only for the major highs and lows, the things you'd like everyone to keep in their hearts or in their prayers for you.

Silence. Each gathering has a time of silence, at least three minutes. Groups may want to build to longer times as group members become accustomed to the silence. Initially, people are often reluctant to give enough time for this silence; but in our society, where silence is so rare, even three minutes of silence can be a precious gift.

Shared Readings. Going around the circle, each person will read a poem or short paragraph, or the leader may ask just one or two people to do the readings. The readings are designed to further deepen and broaden the theme of the gathering.

Sharing. In the first round of sharing, the leader will pose a question related to the topic of the gathering. Going around the circle, everyone will have an opportunity to briefly respond.

After a short silence, you will have a second opportunity to speak. This time each person speaks when ready, not necessarily in order. Your task will be to speak more personally than you did in the first round—to talk about something that touched you, to share feelings, to tell a story about your experience with this topic. The listeners' job is to keep an open heart for what is shared. Everyone should have the opportunity to speak, but anyone may pass.

If there is time for a third round, you may talk more deeply about what you have said or share thoughts sparked by what others have said. Probably not everyone will speak. Although this round is more informal than the first two rounds, it's still not casual chit-chat. It is always appropriate to point out when the group seems to be getting off track.

In our culture, we often believe that we need to prove we have listened by asking an intelligent question about what has been said. But it doesn't always feel good to be asked a lot of questions. Questions may harbor judgment or feel distancing. Sometimes a question can clarify information, but the fewer questions, the better.

You and your group will benefit most if you share as deeply as you can. Take the risk of talking about tender places, half-formed ideas, and feelings you don't yet understand. You'll find that hearing yourself talk about these edges of your awareness will help you continue to grow.

It's up to everyone in the group to help one another feel safe in sharing. One very important way to achieve that safety is by maintaining confidentiality. Avoid gossip, which for our purposes is defined as telling someone else's story with a less than generous spirit. Gossip threatens group bonding and trust. Many groups decide to honor confidentiality of attribution, meaning you can talk about what happens in the group as long as you don't indicate who said what. This allows talking about what happened in the group if there's a good reason and the focus of the sharing is your own story. For instance, telling your partner about an important insight may require revealing something about what has happened in the group. Your group may decide instead to keep absolute confidentiality, meaning that members promise to not discuss anything that happens in the group.

Closing Activity. This is an interactive exercise, a question for people to comment on, or a ritual to help wrap up your time together. The ritual addresses the topic in a different way. The leader will guide you through the ritual.

Closing Words. Every gathering has a reading to reflect upon following the Closing Activity.

Song. Stand in a circle and sing the song "Thank You for Your Loving Hands" by Judy Fjell (page xii). This song is very easy to learn and sing. If you do not read music, it is very likely that someone in your group will be able to teach it to the others.

Announcements. This is an opportunity for the leader to share plans or give reminders to the group, such as what to bring to the next gathering.

Before the First Gathering

Every member of your group should have a copy of this book. Before coming to the gathering, read this introduction, then turn to the Listening gathering (page 1). Read the quotations and the essay, then do one or more of the activities.

THANK YOU FOR YOUR LOVING HANDS

Music: Judy Fjell ©1982   Lyrics: Lisa Bregger & Judy Fjell©2000

Thank you for your loving hands, your lov ing heart your lov ing ways

Thank you for the gifts you bring in - to the world each day And

if you ev - er doubt your self re -mem ber us who love you well

We know all the gifts you bring in - to the world each day So

thank you for your lov ing hands your lov ing heart your lov ing ways

Thank you for the gifts you bring in - to the world each day!

Our Hope for You

You are about to embark on an adventure in community, listening and trust. Our deep hope is that you will find your life enriched by your heart-to-heart group experience, and that you will take what you learn about yourselves and each other out into our fractured and hurting world.

Listening

∿

BEFORE YOU GATHER

We need to be known. This knowledge of being known we call love.
  —Alan Jones

I want to unfold.
Let no place in me hold itself closed,
  —Rainer Maria Rilke

If we want to support each other's inner lives, we must remember a simple truth: the human soul does not want to be fixed, it wants simply to be seen and heard.
  —Parker J. Palmer

We are really alive when we listen to each other, to the silences of each other as well as to the words and what lies behind the words.
  —Frederick Buechner

I believe we can change the world if we start listening to one another again . . . Simple, truthful conversation where we each have a chance to speak, we each feel heard, and we each listen well.
  —Margaret Wheatley

Consider This

We listen to other people a lot. We listen to pass the time, to get information, to be entertained. We listen waiting for our turn to speak. We listen because it is expected of us.

Most of the time we don't listen deeply, even when our intent is to be helpful. We think we are listening, but we are spending most of our energy thinking about things to say that are encouraging or insightful. We are often surprised when our "helpful" comments end the sharing, or when the speaker says, "I don't need you to solve my problem, I just want you to listen!"

Why is it so difficult to just listen? Perhaps because we have a hard time believing that it is simply our presence that helps, rather than our thinking and advising. Our open hearts do the healing rather than our carefully chosen words. But most of us haven't experienced this.

Physician and author Rachel Naomi Remen says, "I suspect that the most basic and powerful way to connect to another person is to listen. Just listen. Perhaps the most important thing we ever give each other is our attention . . . When people are talking, there's no need to do anything but receive them."

The kind of listening you will offer and receive in your group gatherings can be a great blessing to others. The structure of the gatherings will help you learn this unfamiliar discipline. You won't have to think about how to respond to others because that's not part of the process. It may take some getting used to—at first, it can feel uncaring to just listen to someone without commenting or commiserating. But the process can be very supportive. We feel free to say what is in our hearts when we don't have to fend off misunderstandings or clumsy responses.

That doesn't mean the listening is passive. It's hard work to listen with an open heart rather than an analyzing mind. It requires putting aside judgment, categorization, and evaluation and instead just hearing the story that is told, and the feelings behind it. Some people say they can feel themselves shift from their minds to hearts when they are listening. Some describe deep listening as a sacred experience.

It is the mind's nature to think, and so even the most experienced listeners repeatedly will slip into judging and analyzing. When you realize that this has happened, gently set aside your thinking for later and open your heart. Buddhist meditators, who face the same problem, speak of treating the mind like a beloved but sometimes inappropriate child who wants to show off to guests. "Not now, sweetie," says the kind parent. "You go and play and we will join you in a bit." Similarly, when we are listening and notice that we are commenting to ourselves about what is being said, we can tell our minds, "This is not the time for analysis. I just need to hear this story."

Most people need a few experiences of simply being listened to before they can really believe that just listening is enough. In time, we discover that to be listened to is a way of being loved, and that listening is a way of being loving. We can take what we learn from our sharing groups out into the rest of our lives and bless the world.

Activities

Before the group meeting, reflect on the idea of sharing in a group by creating your stepping stones (see below) and choosing one or more of the other journaling suggestions to explore this topic. Also, be sure to read the "Introduction" chapter (page v).

Stepping Stones. To help you begin to tell your story to others in the group, think about your life so far as a set of stepping stones marking major eras in your life. These could include your years as a single mother, or the time you served in the military, or the job you had in Portland, or the time you spent recovering from an accident. Often stepping stones begin or end with a major event of some kind. You might describe one by saying, "I was promoted to a job which I hated and I did it faithfully for three years until I had a heart attack, which was a wake up call, and so I moved on to . . ." Or, "Joey was born and I stayed home with him and earned my degree. I graduated, he turned three, and that era ended."

Start with as many stepping stones as you'd like, but try to collapse them into about five "eras" that you are willing to share with the group.

Journaling Suggestions. What is your favorite childhood story? What is your favorite "victim" story, your favorite "hero" story?

When you were a child, how did your family act around the dinner table? What was mealtime like?

Write about a time in the past few years when you called on one or several of "your communities" for help, nurturing, and support.

Along with your "Stepping Stones" list, bring to the group five tokens such as coins, game markers, pebbles, or similar small items. You can bring five of the same thing, or you can bring tokens that symbolize the five stepping stones of your life.

∞

GATHERING

Candle Lighting

We come together in an attitude of openness—not knowing quite what will happen, yet daring to receive a new idea, a new experience, sustenance for our minds and our hearts.

We come with an attitude of humility, knowing how much we need one another, how alone we can be in the world, how vulnerable if we face life only by ourselves.

We come in the spirit of love, seeking human warmth and fellowship in the hands and faces of those around us.

—Peter Lee Scott

Covenant and Ground Rules

I commit myself:

- to come to meetings when I possibly can, knowing that my presence is important to the group;
- to let the leader know if I will be absent or need to quit;
- to share with the leader the responsibility for good group process by watching how much time I take to speak and noticing what is going on for others;
- to do the reading and thinking about the topic ahead of time;
- to not gossip about what is shared in the group, and tell only my own story to others;
- to honor the safety of the group by listening to what others share with an open heart;
- to refrain from cross-talk, judging, or giving advice;
- to ask questions gently and only if necessary;
- and to share as deeply as I can when it is my turn.

On Our Hearts   10 minutes

Silence   3 minutes

Shared Readings

Each of us brings a separate truth here,
We bring the truth of our own life, our own story.
We don't come as empty vessels . . .
But rather we come as full people—people who have our own
   story and our own truth . . .
Together we have truths.
Together we have a story.
Together we are a community.
   —Penny Hackett-Evans

We have begun to learn about a method of deep listening. As we already know, we have to practice before we can listen deeply. Sometimes we can also translate "deep listening" as compassionate listening, that is, to listen with compassion, or to listen with love. We hear with one aim only; we don't listen in order to criticize, to blame, to correct the person who is speaking or to condemn the person. We only listen with one aim, and that is to relieve the suffering of the one we are listening to.

—Thich Nhat Hanh

Sharing   60 minutes

Closing Activity

Sharing Insights

Closing Words

As we part now one from another, let these be our thoughts:

If that which is most holy lies within the human person, and if the greatest power in the world shines flickering and uncertain from each individual heart, then it is easy to see the value of human associations dedicated to nurturing that light: the couple, the family, the religious community.

For the power of good in any one of us must at times waver. But when a group together is dedicated to nurturing the power of good, it is rare for the light to grow dim in all individuals at the same moment.

So we borrow courage and wisdom from one another, to warm us and keep us until we're together again.

—Eileen Karpeles

Conclude the gathering by singing "Thank You for Your Loving Hands" (page xii) and making any necessary announcements.

Gratitude

∾

BEFORE YOU GATHER

If the only prayer you ever say in your life is "thank you," it will be enough.
— Meister Ekhart

Just to be is a blessing. Just to live is holy.
— Abraham Heschel

A thankful person is thankful under all circumstances. A complaining soul complains even if he lives in paradise.
— Baha'u'llah

To be grateful for the good things that happen in our lives is easy, but to be grateful for all of our lives—the good as well as the bad, the moments of joy as well as the moments of sorrow, the successes as well as the failures, the rewards as well as the rejections—that requires hard spiritual work.
— Henri Nouwen

Consider This

It has been said that religion is primarily an affair of gratitude. You may have always thought that religion is primarily an affair of believing, and if you were not sure how a person goes about "believing," you may have thought you were not a religious person. Gratitude, on the other hand, is something that all of us can practice, and that makes us all religious.

Whatever one's beliefs about faith and grace, gratitude is basic. Like hope, trust, and love, gratitude is both a feeling and a spiritual practice. Though we have little control over our immediate feelings, we can decide to cultivate the ground in which those feelings thrive.

We are taught as soon as we can speak to say "thank you" when we are helped or given something. A young person who does not say "thank you" convincingly is considered spoiled, and an older person who does not have this habit is considered arrogant. Why? Words of thanks signal acknowledgement of another's part in benefiting our lives. "Thank you" adds a human connection. It says, "I noticed you were there, and I am glad."

Our thank-yous remind us that we are dependent on those around us. The words acknowledge the web of relationships in which we live. To neglect one's thank-yous is not only rude; it is out of touch with reality, an implicit claim of independence and privilege. The practice of saying "thank you" is good for our souls and a reality check on our tendency to think we don't need others. This is not only important in our relationships with other people, it is important in our relationship with God, the universe, our life.

When There Is No One to Thank. If you don't believe in a "thankable" God, you may wonder how to develop gratitude. But you don't have to believe that there is a Divine Someone out there collecting praise to experience gratitude. The important thing is to notice your gratitude and express it, if only to yourself. "Thank you, Universe!" you might say, if "Thank you, God" doesn't work for you. We notice our full hearts when a grandchild rushes into our arms, when we are struck by the beauty of a sunset, or when we experience one of those wonderful moments when we connect deeply with someone. There may be nobody in particular to thank, but we can practice gratitude all the same.

When Things Are Awful. Sometimes we are suffering too much to feel honestly grateful. There are days, even weeks or months, when we are overwhelmed by problems or pain, tragedy or disappointment. At those times, we don't feel lucky to be alive and certainly don't feel like celebrating. In their desire to make us feel better, good-hearted people are likely to say things like "You should be grateful that . . ." (your older child is still alive, the cancer was only in one breast, you still have a spouse even though you lost your job). But when we can't feel grateful, we can't. At least, we can't right now. (Note to good-hearted people: You are right, the suffering person in front of you surely still has some good things in his or her life. But this realization has to come from within, and it will come more quickly if friends simply listen with open hearts and don't try to give advice.)

Sometimes when things are hard, especially if they are awful for a long time, we resolve to make a practice of gratitude—to really work at reestablishing our sense of thanksgiving. This is a very healing practice. In the midst of grieving for a loved one, we can be grateful for the care of friends, for the flowers that are still blooming, for the kindness of strangers, or even that the car still starts and the sun still rises. Being intentional about noticing these things is a deep spiritual practice.

The Jewish people have a beloved song that is sung at the Seder, the service that takes place during the Passover season. Passover celebrates the Exodus from Egypt, when Hebrew slaves were freed and escaped into a difficult forty years in the wilderness. In the song, called "Dayeinu," the leader lists all of the things that God did during the Exodus story. After each, the congregation sings "Dayeinu," which means, "It would have been enough." It goes something like this:

Had God brought us out of Egypt
and not divided the sea for us,
    It would have been enough.
Had God divided the sea
and not permitted us to cross on dry land,
    It would have been enough.

Had God permitted us to cross the sea on dry land
and not sustained us for forty years in the desert,
   It would have been enough.

You get the idea. In spite of the considerable suffering involved in an entire community's uprooting itself to escape into the wilderness, there is also gratitude for all the ways things turned out well. "Dayeinu" is a way of saying, "There are gifts even in the midst of this hard time." So a new mother might say to herself:

If my baby had been born healthy, but not beautiful,
   It would have been enough.
If he had been born healthy and beautiful, but I had to struggle to care for him,
   It would have been enough.
If he had been healthy and beautiful, and my mother came to care for us both, but I had to return to a nine-to-five job,
   It would have been enough.
But I have a flexible job, a loving mother, a beautiful and healthy baby, and it is so much more than enough.

Practice Gratitude. Perhaps most insidious to our sense of gratitude is the great demon, busyness. There are times when we simply get too busy to notice all the wonderful things and people and relationships around us. Because it is so easy to get revved up to such a pitch that we neglect to notice our gratitude, it is best to find ways to make gratitude a routine. The child's "God bless Mommy and Daddy and my brother, even though he's a pain," is an elementary but beneficial practice. Sometimes people keep a gratitude list, have a wall of photographs of people and places for which they are grateful, bring their gratitude to mind each morning over their coffee, or begin the evening meal or bedtime prayers by naming something for which they are grateful.

W. H. Auden once wrote that on the dull days of life, we must practice our "scales of rejoicing." A musician practices scales for many lonely hours so that when it comes time to perform, the music will flow naturally from the fingers. Likewise, we can make a practice of our gratitude that will sustain us in both the wonderful and difficult times of our lives.

Activities

Before the gathering, reflect on gratitude by doing one or more of the following activities.

Words of Gratitude. Select a quotation on the subject of gratitude (you can use one from the opening of this chapter or find another one). Write it out in calligraphy (or use a computer, if you prefer), carve it in wood, stitch it in cross-stitch, or illustrate it with a photograph, drawing, or collage made from magazine cutouts.

Wrist Band Gratitude. The opposite of gratitude is complaint, and many of us complain quite a lot. One way to break this habit, touted by Will Bowen in his book *A Complaint Free World*, uses a colorful silicone wristband. Whenever you realize you have just complained, you move the wristband to the other wrist. As a variation, when you notice you're complaining and you move the wristband, see if you can articulate something to be grateful for at that moment. Try this practice in the days leading up to the gathering.

Respond in Gratitude. As you read this adaptation of Psalm 34, consider how you respond to the blessings in your life. Write a few lines about how you encourage gratitude to enter your heart.

How do I know that God is good?
By opening my heart in gratitude and praise
    for all the gifts of life.
By focusing on the astounding intricacy of the world.
By attending to the still, small voices of healing and renewal
    which save me in times of trouble.
And by loving life and honoring that gift,
    speaking truth, doing good, seeking peace.

When I serve the highest I know
    I serve whatever God there is.
The joy of this, no matter what my troubles, will keep me
    whole.
        —Psalm 34, adapted by Christine Robinson

Make a Scale of Rejoicing. A scale has eight notes, each higher than the other. (Think of "do re mi fa sol la ti do" in *The Sound of Music.*) For each note of the scale, write something you are grateful for in your life. Then sing the scale using your words of gratitude. You can sing or chant your scale of gratitude to yourself throughout the day, such as while waiting for a red light to change or oatmeal to boil. This is an especially good exercise in times of difficulty or suffering.

Journaling Suggestions. Make a list of twenty-five things you are grateful for.

What are you most grateful for in your life right now? What keeps you from being more grateful than you are?

Think about the past day. What words of gratitude do you remember saying? Were there moments when you could have expressed your gratitude, but didn't? Think about something you wish you had said to a dear friend, a parent, a child.

How might you start your day if you had gratitude as your spiritual practice? How might you end your day?

Bring a list of twenty-five things you are grateful for (see Journaling Suggestions above). One activity at the gathering will involve reading a few items from your list, so think about whether you want to keep some of them private.

GATHERING

Candle Lighting

Who can make an accounting of gratitude?
For the universe we give thanks, a room of life to stretch us with
   wonder.
For the earth we give thanks, fragment of the stars that is our
   home ...
For life we give thanks, the burning of stars ordered and
   tempered ...
For growth we give thanks, and brotherhood, for all forces that
   enrich us, ways past our knowing, power past our control;
For ages past our sojourn, for eternity in which our days are
   magnified in being lived therein, we give thanks.
   —Kenneth Patton

On Our Hearts   10 minutes

Silence   3 minutes

Shared Readings

May it be delightful, my house;
From my head may it be delightful;
To my feet may it be delightful;
Where I lie may it be delightful;
All above me may it be delightful;
All around me may it be delightful.
   —Navaho chant

Let us give thanks for a bounty of people.
For generous friends with hearts and smiles as bright as their
  blossoms;
For feisty friends as tart as apples;
For continuous friends, who, like scallions and cucumbers, keep
  reminding us that we've had them;
For crotchety friends, as sour as rhubarb and as indestructible;
For handsome friends, who are as gorgeous as eggplants and as
  elegant as a row of corn, and the others, as plain as potatoes
  and as good for you;
For funny friends, who are as silly as Brussels sprouts and as
  amusing as Jerusalem artichokes, and serious friends, as com-
  plex as cauliflowers and as intricate as onions.
For friends as unpretentious as cabbages, as subtle as summer
  squash, as persistent as parsley, as delightful as dill, as endless
  as zucchini, and who, like parsnips, can be counted on to see
  you throughout the winter;
For old friends, nodding like sunflowers in the evening-time, and
  young friends coming on as fast as radishes;
For loving friends, who wind around us like tendrils and hold us,
  despite our blights, wilts, and witherings;
And finally, for those friends now gone, like gardens past that
  have been harvested, and who fed us in their times that we
  might have life thereafter;
For all these we give thanks.
  —Max Coots

This being human is a guest house.
Every morning a new arrival.
A joy, a depression, a meanness,
some momentary awareness comes
As an unexpected visitor.

Welcome and entertain them all!
Even if they're a crowd of sorrows,

who violently sweep your house
empty of its furniture,
still treat each guest honorably.
He may be clearing you out
for some new delight.

The dark thought, the shame, the malice,
meet them at the door laughing,
and invite them in.

Be grateful for whoever comes,
because each has been sent
as a guide from beyond.
     —Mewlana Jalaluddin Rumi, translated by Coleman Barks

Sharing   60 minutes

Closing Activity

Poem of Gratitude

Closing Words

We build on foundations we did not lay.
We warm ourselves at fires we did not light.
We sit in the shade of trees we did not plant.
We drink from wells we did not dig.
We profit from persons we did not know.
We are ever bound in community.
    —Deuteronomy 6:10–12, adapted by Peter Raible

*Conclude the gathering by singing "Thank You for Your Loving Hands"
(page xii) and making any necessary announcements.*

Balance

༄

BEFORE YOU GATHER

On the tightrope of life, only one thing allows us to move forward, and that one thing is balance.
    —Laura Kangas

The butterfly counts not months but moments, and has time enough.
    —Rabindranath Tagore

People with great gifts are easy to find, but symmetrical and balanced ones never.
    —Ralph Waldo Emerson

You must have a room, or a certain hour or so a day, where you don't know what was in the newspapers that morning . . . a place where you can simply experience and bring forth what you are and what you might be.
    —Joseph Campbell

Balance is not better time management, but better boundary management. Balance means making choices and enjoying those choices.
    —Betsy Jacobson

When you stand with your two feet on the ground, you will always keep your balance.

—Lao Tsu

Consider This

When two or more forces or items are in appropriate relationship to each other, so that the whole benefits, that's balance. Whether the items are the deposits and withdrawals in our bank account (where we want the balance to be on the positive side) or the weight we have on our two feet, balanced so that we don't fall, what's important is that all the elements are in that appropriate relationship.

We moderns often feel that our lives are out of balance. In particular, we feel that the necessities of work, commuting, and household chores take up too much time and energy, leaving little for family, creativity, rest, or spiritual life. Being out of balance makes us unhappy, and sometimes even unhealthy.

Life Vision. It's not possible to assess the balance in your life until you have answered the question, "What is my vision for my life?" If your vision is to be a concert musician, you will spend many, many hours alone in a practice room. If your vision is to be a community activist, all that practice time would be completely inappropriate.

Being a "workaholic" is not simply a matter of how many hours are spent at work. When someone begins to own up to the fact that he has become a workaholic, he is realizing that his life's vision includes more than work and that too much work is negatively influencing other values, such as family or health.

An appropriate life vision includes both major and minor factors, and both are important. A young woman may have, as her major vision, being a good mother to her child. Other aspects of her life's vision might include being a responsible community member and continuing to develop her own unique talents.

Emotional Balance. Our sense of having balance in life also depends on our ability to find emotional equilibrium. We find equilibrium in many ways, from a formal meditation practice to a habit of relaxing on the train after work each day, taking our morning coffee to a quiet part of the house, or spending some time with a journal before bed each evening. Being intentional about a Sabbath day each week or attending weekly religious services also gives us time just to be—time when that still, small voice might speak to us about what is important in our lives.

To help us maintain physical balance, the cells in each of our joints continually send information to the brain about the location of every part of the body. Emotional balance requires a similar self-understanding. We must be aware of the levels of stress we live with and notice when they change. When we feel seriously out of balance, we often need information. How many hours do we spend working, being with family, exercising, entertaining ourselves, caring for pets, cooking, shopping? How much money do we really need to live on and save prudently? Is the family schedule really working? Spending a few minutes before bed each evening making notes about how we spent our day can be instructive. Without information, it is hard to make decisions.

Discipline. The muscles we use in balancing our lives are the muscles of discernment and self-discipline. They help us figure out which activities are within our life's vision and what their various levels should be, and then to make decisions based on that discernment. That means we will often say no to requests from others, or even to desires of our own, because we are in touch with our vision.

The muscles of discernment and self-discipline, like physical muscles, are developed by exercise that starts light and gets heavier. If you've never been able to say no to your mother, you can practice by saying no to the bake sale committee chair. If starting to meditate feels like running a marathon, you can start with short periods, or in a class, or on a form of meditation that is particularly congenial to you. These are all ways to strengthen the "core muscles" of balance in your life.

If you can articulate your vision for your life, you'll have a way to figure out how much time and energy to spend on various activities. Then it's a matter of noticing what you're really doing and use your self-discipline to choose a balanced set of activities that are in accord with your vision. Whether that means a sixty-hour work week or dropping everything to tend to an ailing family member, if it's in accord with your vision, you'll enjoy both the reward of your choices and the centeredness that a balanced life brings.

Activities

Before the gathering, reflect on balance by doing one or more of the following activities.

Vision of the Future. If you're not sure what your life's vision is, try this. Imagine that you are an elderly person and it is your birthday. A party is being held, and people from all the important facets of your life—family, friends, work, community—are coming to honor you.

Write about what happens at this birthday party. Who is there? What do they say about the quality of your character, your accomplishments, your activities, and the difference you made in the world? What do they say about your habits of living, your activities, your foibles?

In this imaginary scenario, combine what has already happened in your life with what you hope for. For instance, you may not yet have children or have written the great American novel, but if those are some of your life's goals, go ahead and imagine that they have happened.

Review of the Day. How do you really spend your time? For the next week, each evening before you go to bed, take a few minutes to list your major activities for the day in categories. For instance:

- Sleep: 7.5 hours
- Grooming: 45 minutes (30 in the morning, 15 in the evening)
- Exercise: 1 hour, 15 minutes (30 minutes of actual exercise, plus travel to gym and changing)
- Work: 9.5 hours (8 at work, 1 hour commuting, a half-hour of email in the evening)
- Volunteering: (none today)
- Food and home chores: 3 hours
- Spiritual life: 1.5 hours (30 minutes in morning and an hour's talk with a friend)
- Family: 30 minutes (phoned Mom)

What did you learn from this activity? Did your list include any "time eaters" that surprised you?

The Rooms in Your Life. Here's an activity suggested by Erica Orloff and Kathy Levinson in their book *Walking the Tightrope: Solutions for Achieving Life Balance Without a Net.* Imagine your life as a house. Each room represents a different area of your life, and the size of the room indicates how much time you spend on that area. For instance, if your job takes up most of your day and part of the evening, the room representing "job" will be sizable. If you find you are spending very little time on family and friends, that room will be tiny.

With this in mind, draw a floor plan of a house that represents how you spend your time. Use the following guidelines to determine the size of the rooms. (If one of the categories doesn't apply to you, simply leave that room out.)

- Kitchen: All the time you spend on the chores of your life: cooking and cleaning, shopping, yard care, toting kids around, and so on
- Bathroom: The time you spend on health appointments, exercise routines, bathing, and other care of your body
- Living room: Time spent with friends and family (excluding your spouse or partner)

- Media room: Entertainment time (computer games, TV, music, travel)
- Bedroom 1: Sleep
- Bedroom 2: Time spent with your significant other—not just sex, but communication and hanging out together
- Bedroom 3: Kids' time
- Workshop: Hobbies and creative time
- Garage: Time spent at your job
- Closet or study: "Me" time, spiritual life
- Shed: Volunteer/community work

When you're finished, take a look at your house. What issues of balance jump out at you? What changes would you have to make to grow toward a more ideal life balance?

See-Saw Diagram. Draw a simple see-saw, with one end resting on the ground and the other in the air. Think about what you have too much of in your life (that which is weighing you down). Put words or symbols to represent those elements on the "down" side of the see-saw. On the "up" side, put those elements that you do not have enough of.

Return to this activity over several days as you think of other aspects of your life. What do you need to add more of in your life to achieve better balance? What areas take over? What gets crowded out?

Walking Meditation. Try this practice, from a book called *The Long Road Turns to Joy: A Guide to Walking Meditation* by Buddhist monk Thich Nhat Hanh:

> Walking meditation is meditation while walking. We walk slowly, in a relaxed way, keeping a light smile on our lips. When we practice this way, we feel deeply at ease, and our steps are those of the most secure person on Earth. All our sorrows and anxieties drop away, and peace and joy fill our hearts. Anyone can do it. It takes only a little time, a little mindfulness, and the wish to be happy. . . .

We can practice walking meditation by counting steps or by using words. If the rhythm of our breathing is three steps for each in-breath and out-breath (3-3), for example, we can say, silently, "Lotus flower blooms. Lotus flower blooms," or "The green planet. The green planet," as we walk. If our breathing is two steps for each in-breath, and three steps for each out breath (2-3), we might say, "Lotus flower. Lotus flower blooms." ...

We don't just say the words. We really see flowers blooming under our feet. We really become one with our green planet. Feel free to use your own creativity and wisdom. Walking meditation is not hard labor. It is for your enjoyment. ...

(When you begin to practice walking meditation, you might feel unbalanced, like a baby learning to walk. Follow your breathing, dwell mindfully on your steps, and soon you will find your balance. Visualize a tiger walking slowly, and you will find that your steps become as majestic as the steps of a tiger.)

Journaling Suggestions. On a scale of one to ten (ten is a good score), how happy are you with the balance in your life? Why?

Consider different areas of your life, such as work, leisure, rest, family and friends, solitary times, security, vision/dreams, spiritual health, physical health, and so on. What is there too much of in your life? What is there not enough of in your life?

If one aspect of your life is throwing things off balance, dialogue with that area about your concerns. For instance, if you feel time spent on the computer is out of balance, you might dialogue this way:

Me: I am concerned that I spend too much time on email.

Computer: How often do you check email?

Me: It just shows up, so I check whenever a new message comes in.

Computer: Hmm, what if you . . .

Take a journey into the future, six months from now. What would your day look like in the future if you had worked today to achieve better balance in your life? What would you have more of? Less of?

What holds you back from making changes? What is one balance adjustment you are willing to try out?

Think about the areas of your life that seem out of balance. Jot down a few that you are willing to share with the group.

∾

GATHERING

Candle Lighting

Out of our busyness, we are called back into balance, back into ourselves and the silence of present being. But it is not just back into ourselves to which we are called; it is also to the awareness of the continuous presence of the environment around us and within us. We are called to remember our relationships and our dependencies. We are called to once again feel the oneness which sustains our being in balance with creation, and to do so with wonder and appreciation.

—Susan Manker-Seale

On Our Hearts   10 minutes

Silence   3 minutes

Shared Readings

Just as your car runs more smoothly and requires less energy to go faster and farther when the wheels are in perfect alignment, you perform better when your thoughts, feelings, emotions, goals, and values are in balance.
  —Brian Tracy

We spend January 1 walking through our lives, room by room, drawing up a list of work to be done, cracks to be patched. Maybe this year, to balance the list, we ought to walk through the rooms of our lives . . . not looking for flaws, but for potential.
  —Ellen Goodman

Wisdom is your perspective on life, your sense of balance, your understanding of how the various parts and principles apply and relate to each other. It embraces judgment, discernment, comprehension. It is a gestalt or oneness, and integrated wholeness.
  —Stephen R. Covey

Sharing   60 minutes

Closing Activity

Coming into Balance

Closing Words

The best and safest thing is to keep a balance in your life, acknowledge the great powers around us and in us. If you can do that, and live that way, you are really a wise man.
  —Euripides

Conclude the gathering by singing "Thank You for Your Loving Hands" (page xii) and making any necessary announcements.

Forgiveness

∾

BEFORE YOU GATHER

We must be saved by the final form of love, which is forgiveness.
—Reinhold Niebuhr

The weak can never forgive. Forgiveness is the attribute of the strong.
—Mahatma Gandhi

Forgiveness is not an emotion, it's a decision.
—Randall Worley

If you wish to travel far and fast, travel light. Take off all your envies, jealousies, unforgiveness, selfishness, and fears.
—Glenn Clark

Never does the human soul appear so strong as when it foregoes revenge, and dares forgive an injury.
—E. H. Chapin

Forgiveness is me giving up my right to hurt you for hurting me.
—Anonymous

To err is human; to forgive, divine.
—Alexander Pope

We are told that people stay in love because of chemistry, or because they remain intrigued with each other, because of many kindnesses, because of luck. . . . But part of it has got to be forgiveness and gratefulness.
　—Ellen Goodman

Forgiveness is not an occasional act; it is a permanent attitude.
　—Dr. Martin Luther King Jr.

Consider This

Suppose my neighbor's dog escaped his yard, came into mine, and killed my child's cat. I'm not only grieving the cat and suffering with my grieving child, I'm furious! When someone has hurt me, I have a right to be angry.

But exercising that right, it turns out, only keeps the hurt alive. It means that every time I see that neighbor, I'm stabbed again with grief for my pet and fury at his dog. I lose a good neighbor and a sense of ease in my neighborhood. It's just not worth it. Ironically, the only way to restore ease in my life and keep this neighbor and his dog from hurting me over and over is to forgive.

Forgiving is letting go of the right to be angry in service of health and wholeness. If this were easy to do, it wouldn't be necessary for all the world's religions to emphasize forgiveness. But it is not easy. Indeed, it is the most difficult emotional and spiritual move human beings learn to make.

Since forgiveness involves our emotional life, we are not in complete control of the process. We cannot force ourselves to forgive, no matter how strongly we believe that we should. All we can do is lean ourselves into being willing to forgive, and our forgiveness—the fading of our anger—will come in its own time.

Sometimes we are so angry and hurt that we can only hope or pray for the desire to be willing to forgive. But even that means we are on the path of forgiveness, and that's a step toward the health and healing we need in our lives. This path can be made easier by understanding forgiveness properly.

Forgiveness Is Not Pardon. To pardon is to gloss over an offense as if it didn't matter. Pardon is a move for politicians who have no personal stake in the matter. The idea of pardon is an outrage to the hurt.

In contrast to pardon, forgiveness begins by acknowledging the hurt, and only then explores the possibility of giving up the anger and continuing the relationship in spite of the offense. Forgiveness does not say, "That didn't matter." Forgiveness says, "That really hurt, and it really harmed our relationship, but I don't want to be angry about it any more."

Forgiveness Is Not Reconciliation. Forgiveness and reconciliation are not quite the same. Forgiveness happens when we let go of our anger toward someone who has hurt us. Forgiveness can be one-sided; it need not be reciprocated by the other person. Therefore we can forgive a person who has died or whom we will never see again. We can forgive those who insist that they had a right to do what they did to hurt us. We can even, in extreme cases, forgive a person who is continuing to hurt us in ways we cannot prevent.

We can forgive on our own, but it takes two to reconcile. Reconciliation happens when both parties forgive each other and decide to continue the relationship in some form that feels safe to both of them.

Feeling safe in a relationship does not happen just because we give up our anger. We must give some thought to how we can feel safe again. If your confidence has been betrayed, you might forgive the gossiper and continue a friendly relationship, but you will probably be somewhat guarded for a while. If your child has stolen money from your wallet, you will certainly want to continue the relationship, but you might keep your wallet out of temptation's way. Making those decisions is a part of reconciliation.

Forgiving and Forgetting. Sometimes we think we've forgiven someone (or that we should forgive him or her), but find ourselves continuing to bring up the hurt over and over again. That's a big clue that we have not actually forgiven or have not found a way to be safe in the relationship. We have more work to do.

But forgiving does not require forgetting. Indeed, our memory of past hurts is one of the things that helps us stay safe in the future. We just need to find a way to give up our anger so that when we remember the incident, the sting is gone, and all that is left is what we learned. Then we can continue the relationship.

Once we have gotten to that point, the incident or hurt will begin to fade in importance, and we won't think of it so much or be tempted to bring it up. We can make changes that allow us to move forward in a relationship. For instance, my dog-owning neighbor might mend his fence, and I might vow to make my next cat an indoor cat. These agreements make it possible for the two of us to co-exist safely again. As we continue the relationship, we'll begin to amass new experiences that will be much more "front and center" in our memories. That's the "forgetting" of forgiveness.

Tasks of Forgiveness. Forgiveness is a process, not an event. While we can't control our feelings, we can set ourselves to the tasks that are essential to the process.

The first task of forgiveness is to honor the fact that we have been hurt, and not try to sweep it under the rug. If we tell ourselves "It was nothing" but seethe inwardly, we will never be able to forgive. When we acknowledge the hurt to ourselves and come to understand what part of ourselves was hurt, we've started the process of healing.

Our next task is to hear or imagine the other person's side, holding our hearts as open as we possibly can to the other person's reality and motivations. The friend who was so late to meet you may come from a family that views time and lateness very differently from yours. Your dog-owning neighbor may tell you something new—that he had no idea his dog had learned to open the gate, and that a dog-proof latch has now been installed. The co-worker who betrayed your confidence may be sincerely sorry. If you consider your deceased father's life and all he had to cope with, along with what your uncle tells you about their childhood, you begin to understand why he was as he was. It doesn't cure the hurt, for you will still wish he had been able to give you more, but it helps.

Next, we must step out of our self-righteousness and remember that we are not perfect ourselves and come to terms with the ways we might have contributed to the problem. Usually these steps go a long way to develop our willingness to forgive.

Reconciliation. Now we can move from the internal process of forgiveness to the relational process of reconciliation. We must ask ourselves if we want to continue the relationship and, if necessary, what we will need to feel safe in that. One way to get the ball rolling is to apologize for what we can. "You know," I say to my dog-owning neighbor, "I realize that this has been hard for you, too, and I'm sorry for that. I thought cats could protect themselves from dogs. I'm going to have indoor cats from now on." "Well, I have just felt terrible about the whole thing," says the neighbor. "I've had dogs die, and I know how that hurts. I try to keep my yard fenced but the dog will dig. I've been inspecting it once a week or so. And I did hate the idea of this being between us." We are well on our way, not only to forgiveness but to reconciliation.

The final task is to envision how the relationship might go forward. You might agree to meet your tardy friend for lunch again, but with the caveat that she will give you a call when she actually leaves her house.

Lifting the Burden. In the story collection *What If Nobody Forgave?* Barbara Marshman tells a sweet story about the land of Grudgeville, where nobody ever forgives anybody. The people are bent to the ground under the weight of bulging backpacks and heavy packages, which represent their anger, resentment, and grudges. They can see nothing but the ground beneath their feet, and there is no joy in their lives. A stranger comes to town and tells them that it is really not necessary for them to suffer so, that all they must do is say "I am sorry" and "I forgive you." As the townspeople begin to mutter these words, the burdens fall off their backs, and they can straighten up and live free for the first time in generations.

We know that there is considerable work to get to the point of being able to utter these two phrases. But the picture of liberation in the story reminds us of the great value of forgiveness. The work of forgiveness is the work of healing, which restores us when we have been hurt and allows us to continue our lives, free of the corrosive effects of anger and resentment.

Activities

Before the gathering, reflect on forgiveness by doing one or more of the following activities.

The Parable of the Lost Son. In his book *Everything Belongs*, Richard Rohr states that two-thirds of Jesus's sayings were on forgiveness. The best of them is the story of the prodigal son, found in Luke. Read the story (below) and ask yourself: What parts of you are the forgiving father, the wayward son, and the responsible, self-righteous son?

> There was a man who had two sons. The younger of them said to his father, "Father, give me the share of the property that will belong to me." So he divided his property between them. A few days later the younger son gathered all he had and traveled to a distant country, and there he squandered his property in dissolute living. When he had spent everything, a severe famine took place throughout that country, and he began to be in need. So he went and hired himself out to one of the citizens of that country, who sent him to his fields to feed the pigs. He would gladly have filled himself with the pods that the pigs were eating; and no one gave

him anything. But when he came to himself he said, "How many of my father's hired hands have bread enough and to spare, but here I am dying of hunger! I will get up and go to my father, and I will say to him, "Father, I have sinned against heaven and before you; I am no longer worthy to be called your son; treat me like one of your hired hands.'" So he set off and went to his father. But while he was still far off, his father saw him and was filled with compassion; he ran and put his arms around him and kissed him. Then the son said to him, "Father, I have sinned against heaven and before you; I am no longer worthy to be called your son." But the father said to his slaves, "Quickly, bring out a robe—the best one—and put it on him; put a ring on his finger and sandals on his feet. And get the fatted calf and kill it, and let us eat and celebrate; for this son of mine was dead and is alive again; he was lost and is found!" And they began to celebrate.

Now his elder son was in the field; and when he came and approached the house, he heard music and dancing. He called one of the slaves and asked what was going on. He replied, "Your brother has come, and your father has killed the fatted calf, because he has got him back safe and sound." Then he became angry and refused to go in. His father came out and began to plead with him. But he answered his father, "Listen! For all these years I have been working like a slave for you, and I have never disobeyed your command; yet you have never given me even a young goat so that I might celebrate with my friends. But when this son of yours came back, who has devoured your property with prostitutes, you killed the fatted calf for him!" Then the father said to him, "Son, you are always with me, and all that is mine is yours. But we had to celebrate and rejoice, because this brother of yours was dead and has come to life; he was lost and has been found."

—Luke 15:11–32

Meditate on Forgiveness. One line in the Lord's Prayer is often translated as "Forgive us our sins, as we forgive those who sin against us." Below are several other possible translations by biblical scholar Neil Douglas Klotz in his book *Prayers of the Cosmos.* If one of these phrases speaks to you, use it as a prayer phrase or a mantra, which is a meaningful phrase repeated over and over. Do this several times during the week and let it work on you. Alternatively, print it out and tape it to your mirror, or make it your screen saver.

- Loose the cords of mistakes binding us, as we release the strands we hold of others' guilt.
- Forgive our hidden past, the secret shames, as we consistently forgive what others hide.
- Compost our inner stolen fruit as we forgive others the spoils of their trespassing.
- Untangle the knots within so that we can mend our hearts' simple ties to others.
- Erase the inner marks our failures make, just as we scrub our hearts of others' faults.

Write a Dialogue. If there is someone in your life from whom you feel estranged, try writing a dialogue with that person. Begin by asking what he or she experienced. Then tell the person what you experienced. Ask why the person did what he or she did. Ask whether the person understands why you did what you did.

For instance, it might begin like this:

Me: Tell me what you think happened between us.

The other person: Well I . . . and you . . .

Me: Here's how it was for me. I . . . and you . . .

Me: Why did you do . . .

The other person: Because . . .

Write a Letter. If there is someone in your life whom you are willing to forgive, but who is no longer available to you because of death or distance, write the person a letter. Tell the person about what happened, how it affected you, and why you want to forgive him or her. Write about what you imagine was going on with the person. You can keep the letter or make a ceremony of burning it.

Talk It Out. This gathering might bring to mind truly serious hurts that have not yet healed or even been acknowledged. If that's the case for you, this could be a fruitful topic to take to a counselor or spiritual advisor. Even one session of talking things out with a professional can often be very helpful. Your clergyperson, a pastoral counseling center, or friends who are in the "listening" professions can refer you to someone who can listen to your story in more detail than your group can. Remember, the first step of forgiveness is acknowledging and dealing with the hurt. If this is your road, may it be fruitful.

Journaling Suggestions. Take a few moments to think about your "forgiveness history" and make two lists: Whom have you forgiven and for what? Who has forgiven you?

Write about a childhood incident that taught you (for good or for ill) about forgiveness.

How well are you able to forgive yourself?

A Chinese proverb says, "Before you start on the road to revenge, dig two graves." What or who would be buried in the two graves? Who is the winner once revenge enters the scene? Describe a time when you were motivated by revenge or realized that revenge was part of the way you handled a situation.

Think about some of the situations of forgiveness that you are working on in your life, what you are willing to share, and how you would like to share with your group. It is not necessary to reveal names or specific details; you may want to use general terms, like "someone" or "a person in my life."

GATHERING

Candle Lighting

May God—the mind that sees our faults, the tears that sting our wounds, the laugh that soothes our aches, and the love that redeems us all—be illuminated by the light we kindle.
   —Max Coots

On Our Hearts   10 minutes

Silence   3 minutes

Shared Readings

Forgiveness is not the misguided act of condoning irresponsible, hurtful behavior. Nor is it a superficial turning of the other cheek that leaves us feeling victimized and martyred. Rather it is the finishing of old business that allows us to experience the present, free of contamination from the past.
   —Joan Borysenko

The choice to follow love through to its completion is the choice to seek completion within ourselves. The point at which we shut down on others is the point at which we shut down on life. We heal as we heal others, and we heal others by extending our perceptions past their weaknesses. Until we have seen someone's darkness, we don't really know who that person is. Until we have forgiven someone's darkness, we don't really know what love is. Forgiving others is the only way to forgive ourselves, and forgiveness is our greatest need.
   —Marianne Williamson

Sharing   60 minutes

Announcements   5 minutes

Closing Activity

Lighting Candles of Forgiveness

Closing Words

For remaining silent when a single voice would have made a difference

We forgive ourselves and each other; we begin again in love.

For each time that our fears have made us rigid and inaccessible

We forgive ourselves and each other; we begin again in love.

For each time that we have struck out in anger without just cause

We forgive ourselves and each other; we begin again in love.

For each time that our greed has blinded us to the needs of others

We forgive ourselves and each other; we begin again in love.

For the selfishness which sets us apart and alone

We forgive ourselves and each other; we begin again in love.

For falling short of the admonitions of the spirit

We forgive ourselves and each other; we begin again in love.

For losing sight of our unity

We forgive ourselves and each other; we begin again in love.

For those and for so many acts both evident and subtle which have fueled the illusion of separateness

We forgive ourselves and each other; we begin again in love.

—Robert Eller-Isaacs

God

∾

BEFORE YOU GATHER

God enters by a private door into every individual.
   —Ralph Waldo Emerson

You cannot speak of ocean to a well-frog, the creature of a narrower sphere. You cannot speak of ice to a summer insect, the creature of a season.
   —Chuang Tzu

I'm always reluctant to use the word, God, because everybody seems to carry around his own stagnant images and definitions that totally cloud the ability to step outside a narrow, individual frame of reference. If we have any conception of what God is, certainly it should be changing and expanding as we ourselves grow and change.
   —Bernadette Roberts

God, I can push the grass apart
And lay my finger on Thy heart!
   —Edna St. Vincent Millay

Tell me, what is God? He is the breath inside the breath.
   —Kabir (translated by Stephen Mitchell)

If triangles made a god, they would give him three sides.
—Charles de Montesquieu

God is not a person, God is a force. . . . Truth is God.
—Mahatma Gandhi

In music, in the sea, in a flower, in a leaf, in an act of kindness . . .
I see what people call God in all these things.
—Pablo Casals

Our concept of God must be extended as the dimensions of our
world are extended.
—Teihard de Chardin

The atheist staring from his attic window is often nearer to God
than the believer caught up in his own false image of God.
—Martin Buber

Consider This

Almost all of us, even if we don't believe in God, have a mental
image of what that word means. It might be a mysterious figure
in heaven keeping track of good and bad behavior. It might be
an image from scripture: the caring shepherd or the voice in a
whirlwind. It might be a feeling: the lifting of burdens, the gentle
touch of love, or the pricking of conscience. Our picture might
be quite abstract: Great Spirit, Higher Power. We may believe that
our image of God exists (theism), doesn't exist (atheism), or is not
possible to know (agnosticism), but we all have a picture of God
in our minds.

Beyond Words. Orthodox Jews do not use the word *God.* When
speaking aloud, they use a description like "the holy one," and when
writing, they write *G-d.* They do that to remind themselves that this
word signifies more than a mere word can signify—that we can't

ever completely understand the nature of God. For a similar reason, it is often useful to think of "god"—God in quotation marks.

God is not among the things of the world that can be studied by the tools of science and reason or written about with precision. Our experiences of God are interior, subjective experiences. We see "through a glass, darkly," as the Bible says. While we must use words to communicate with others or even think within our own brains, those words only point vaguely at our experience. Therefore, when we speak of our experience and our musings, we should remind ourselves that our words are more art than science, more poetry than prose, and that they must be translated to be understood, if at all, by others.

Why use the word *God* at all, if it is such a slippery thing as to need warnings and explanations? Simply because without words, we can't even think, much less communicate. An example of this phenomenon is found in an isolated culture of hunter-gatherers in New Zealand that uses the same word for the colors blue and green. Because of this, they have great difficulty when presented with the task of sorting blue and green objects by color. They are born with eyes like ours, capable of seeing blue and green as different colors. But without words for the different colors, they don't really "see" them. It is the same for us. As difficult as this word *God* is, if we don't use it (or a good substitute), we'll not be able to think about a part of our lives that most people intuit as existing.

If the word God is spoiled beyond redemption for us, we can substitute other words, such as *Goddess, Higher Power, the Divine, Theos,* or *Great Spirit*. Some people use the word *Goddess* in conversation, as in, "We'll have to leave that to the Goddess." This is not simply a matter of cherishing the feminine connotations of the word, which are often lacking in our "god" words; it is also a way of alerting listeners to the possibility that theological creativity is allowed in this conversation.

It is useful to remember that our images of God, while useful and necessary, are at best partial truths and will lead us astray if taken too literally or set too concretely in our minds. We must each find the definitions, images, and poetry that make sense to us. So here are but a few of the ways God is thought about by many religious people in the world.

Pagan Ideas of Divinity. Generally speaking, pagan theologies such as pantheism, panentheism, and Goddess worship place special emphasis on this earth, this life, and the sacredness of life, our bodies, and the natural world. Pantheists believe that God is the sum total of everything, material and immaterial, in our universe. In this view, everything is holy, even things we might think are not good, such as the lightning that strikes and kills our favorite tree. Panentheism says that God is *in* everything, but is also present beyond the material universe. There are as many definitions of Goddess as of God, but all Goddess theologies explicitly acknowledge and honor the feminine. Traditional, indigenous faiths the world over speak of a *Great Spirit* or a *Mother Goddess.* Modern neo-paganism has attempted to reclaim these definitions of divinity, which had been discredited by patriarchal philosophy and religion over the ages.

A Higher Power. In an attempt to bring spirituality into their programs without entangling people in theological arguments, 12-Step programs such as Alcoholics Anonymous use the term *Higher Power* to denote a divine force that can be defined in many ways. Many people use this term to express a kind of power that exists outside of us, but is mostly manifest within us, and encourages us to become our own higher selves. This higher power is the force that many experience when in dire straits, whether from addiction, illness, grief, or fear, and which gives access to strength, wisdom, and peace that seems to come as a gift from outside ourselves.

Divine Power with Limits. People often think of God as all-powerful. But this raises a serious theological issue, sometimes called the problem of evil: If God is good and all-powerful, why do bad things happen to good people? To resolve this issue, most religions consider divine power to be limited. Orthodox Western religions maintain that God's power is limited by human free will. For instance, God cannot prevent us from deciding to do evil. Some theologies say that the divine being who created the world also created the laws of nature, and those laws limit divine power. God could not have prevented the earthquake or the accident, as these tragedies proceeded according to the laws of nature. Persons who believe that God's power to control events is limited often take solace in the thought that, while God could not prevent their difficulties, God's comforting spirit is with them in those difficulties. Finally, many people believe in a God or transcendent force that has persuasive power over our consciences rather than power over material things like viruses or tornadoes. These are the people who might say, "God has only our hands to do good in the world."

The God of Liberation. The God of liberation theology desires each person to have the maximum possible opportunity for a fully human life. This is a God who sides with the poor and oppressed wherever they are found and nudges all people toward acting for justice and making peace. Liberation theology began as a Catholic movement in Central and South America.

The Human as the Highest. Humanists believe that the highest and best we can know in this universe is humanity, with our grand ideals, marvelous minds, and great potential. They say that divinity is within the human being and nowhere else. Most humanists don't like to use the word God, but they still have a theology, which is a theory or a belief about the highest and best.

The Unfinished God. In process theology, a twentieth-century British-American development, the essence of the divine is creativity. Divinity is that which brings the new into the world, not only through the creation of the universe but through evolution, new ideas, and greater love of humanity.

Atheists and Agnostics. Some people look as deeply and clearly as they know how into life and its meanings and find no hint of a God by any definition, anywhere. They find that the laws of nature and human nature provide satisfying answers to their questions and experiences. They have "no need of that hypothesis," as the mathematician and astronomer Laplace reportedly said to Napoleon. They may feel a sense of freedom and joy that this natural world and the people in it are sufficient to the needs of the day and that the intricacies of the world provide plenty of discovery and meaning for a richly lived human life. If they are quite sure that there is no God, they are atheists. If they feel they don't know for sure but lean against believing, they are agnostics.

Living with Many Names. Many images and understandings of divinity can be found in the world's scriptures, poetry, and theologies. How do we all get along? How can we talk to each other when the meanings behind our words are so different? We do that by being always mindful that our images and understandings are at best approximations of an infinite truth that simply cannot be captured by finite beings. When we remember that fact, our regard for persons with visions and words that differ from ours is not a grudging tolerance but an open-hearted curiosity about yet another way of understanding the divine.

Activities

Before the gathering, reflect on God by doing one or more of the following activities.

Images of the Divine. Images of the divine are found in the Hebrew and Christian scriptures. Read a few—they may expand or cast a new light on your vocabulary for the divine.

Light: The LORD is my light and my salvation. (Psalm 27:1)

Potter: O LORD . . . we are the clay, and you are our potter; we are all the work of your hand. (Isaiah 64:8)

Fortress: My refuge and my fortress; my God, in whom I trust. (Psalm 91:2)

Our dwelling place: Lord, you have been our dwelling-place in all generations. (Psalm 90:1)

Lovingkindness: Blessed be the LORD . . . my lovingkindness. (Psalm 144:1–2, New American Standard Bible)

Spirit of wisdom and understanding: The spirit of the LORD shall rest on him, the spirit of wisdom and understanding. (Isaiah 11:2)

Hiding place: You are a hiding-place for me; you preserve me from trouble; you surround me with glad cries of deliverance. (Psalm 32:7)

Spirit of truth: The Spirit of truth who comes from the Father, he will testify on my behalf. (John 15:26)

Write a Psalm. Read the psalm below and the adaptation that follows it. Then try your hand at writing your own version. Make it personal to your life.

O LORD, you have searched me and known me.
You know when I sit down and when I rise up;
    you discern my thoughts from far away.
You search out my path and my lying down,
    and are acquainted with all my ways.
Even before a word is on my tongue,
    O LORD, you know it completely.
You hem me in, behind and before,
    and lay your hand upon me.
Such knowledge is too wonderful for me;
    it is so high that I cannot attain it.

Where can I go from your spirit?
    Or where can I flee from your presence?
If I ascend to heaven, you are there;
    if I make my bed in Sheol, you are there.
If I take the wings of the morning
    and settle at the farthest limits of the sea,
even there your hand shall lead me,
    and your right hand shall hold me fast.
If I say, "Surely the darkness shall cover me,
    and the light around me become night,"
even the darkness is not dark to you;
    the night is as bright as the day,
    for darkness is as light to you.
    —Psalm 139:1–12

You are closer to me than I am, God
    You shine through from my innermost self.
You know my weak points and my hurt places,
    the habits I resort to and the goals that sustain me.
You well up in me and you hold me in the palm of your hand.

I can't quite grasp this—it's just too big.
    Understanding stays just outside of my focus.
But you're in all of this from the big bang to
    the edge of the cosmos
    From the Beginning to the edge of space and time.
You are in the seed at my center from before my birth, to my
death and beyond
    deep in every growing bone, every forming love, every
    struggled thought.

There is nowhere that you are not.
Search me, try me, purify me
Lead me to the way of Oneness with you.
    —Psalm 139, adapted by Christine Robinson

Concepts of God. Use pictures, symbols, or a few words to represent concepts you have had of God over your lifetime. Show what concepts you had, starting when you were a child, and when and how they changed. What is your concept of God today? What has the transition been like as you have moved from the concept you had in childhood to the concept you have now?

Journaling Suggestions. Make a short list of some beliefs you have had about God in your life (for example, God keeps lists of sins, God is all powerful, God is love). Go back over your list and add some symbols: + or − for beliefs that were positive or negative effects on your life, !! or ?? for beliefs that were very strong or beliefs that you now question, X for beliefs you now reject, and a circle around those that you still embrace.

Which idea of God described in the essay is most in line with your experience of the divine? If none of them fits your experience, what definition would you add to the essay?

What word (if any) do you use to name the divine? Why have you chosen this word?

Where and how is the Sacred revealed to you? Have you had an experience with the Holy? What is that like for you?

Think about the definition of God that most speaks to you. Consider what you are willing to share with the group and how to express this.

∽

GATHERING

Candle Lighting

We bow unto the Light Divine that burns within every living soul.
    —Hindu chant

On Our Hearts   10 minutes

Silence   3 minutes

Shared Readings

The name of this infinite and inexhaustible depth and ground of all being is God. That depth is what the word God means. And if that word has not much meaning for you, translate it, and speak of the depths of your life, of the source of your being, of your ultimate concern, of what you take seriously without any reservation. Perhaps, in order to do so, you must forget everything traditional that you have learned about God, perhaps even that word itself.
    —Paul Tillich

Waiting
Moving beyond one mask
Of God to another
Waiting, with no hope or plan
Waiting in the still void.

Waiting in the desert darkness
No tree to lean against
Or cool water to sip
Waiting for the unknown.

Waiting, not adoration
Waiting, not anticipation
Flat line waiting,
Silence can feel like death.

Loss of the old God
Waiting, wailing, wondering
Waiting through the emptiness
For a shift in the landscape.
    —Alicia Hawkins

The Tao that can be told
Is not the eternal Tao.
The name that can be named
Is not the eternal Name.
  —*Tao te Ching*, translated by Stephen Mitchell

Sharing   60 minutes

Closing Activity

Sharing Insights or Feelings

Closing Words

A person will worship something—have no doubt about that. We
may think our tribute is paid in secret or in the dark recesses of our
hearts—but it will out. That which dominates our imaginations
and our thoughts will determine our lives, and character. Therefore, it behooves us to be careful what we worship, for what we are
worshiping we are becoming.

  —attributed to Ralph Waldo Emerson

*Conclude the gathering by singing "Thank You for Your Loving Hands"
(page xii) and making any necessary announcements.*

Loss and Grief

∾

BEFORE YOU GATHER

To be human is to know loss, and, indeed, the more fully human we are, the more loss we will know and the deeper we will feel the losses; for the more we love and care, the more we have to lose.
  —William Murry

A garden is always a series of losses set against a few triumphs, like life itself.
  —May Sarton

As we experience such a grief, we are drawn out of our normal functioning and thrust into a world and a part of ourselves that is very unfamiliar terrain.
  —Tom Golden

Grief is like a long valley, a winding valley where any bend may reveal a totally new landscape.
  —C. S. Lewis

We want to live like trees . . .
dappled with scars, still exuberantly budding.
  —Adrienne Rich

And even in our sleep pain that cannot forget falls drop by drop upon the heart, and in our own despair, against our will, comes wisdom to us by the awful grace of God.
—Aeschylus

I have found a mourning process for oneself as one gets older and must come to terms with change resulting from this unavoidable progression. One might describe this process as mourning for former states of the self, as if these states represented lost objects.
—George Pollock

At several points in our life we will have to relinquish a former self-image and move on.
—Judith Viorst

Whenever any kind of deep loss occurs in your life—such as loss of possessions, your home, a close relationship; or loss of your reputation, job, or physical abilities—something inside you dies. You feel diminished in your sense of who you are. There may also be a certain disorientation. "Without this . . . who am I?"
—Eckhart Tolle

Consider This

There are many kinds of grief in our lives. When we think of grief, we most often think of the bereaved mother mourning the death of a young soldier, or a widower grieving for his spouse of many years. But actually, we grieve all kinds of losses in our lives. Friends leave town, we grow out of old pastimes, pets die, cherished belongings are destroyed or stolen, we lose jobs, we move to a new home or city, we become unable, through aging or injury, to use our bodies in the same ways. All changes in our lives, even welcome ones, come with attendant losses.

It's tempting to just stuff our painful feelings away, but here is a secret of life: To live fully and joyfully, we have to grieve our losses as they come. Not only does that keep grief from building up, but our small grievings are practice for the big ones: when we must let go of a life dream, when someone close to us dies, when we ourselves face losing our life.

The Tasks of Grief. Grieving is the process of adjusting to loss. In our grieving, we have two tasks: to re-form our sense of self without what we lost, and to internalize our relationship with what used to be physically present.

When we grieve, we have lost more than a person or a thing; we have lost a part of ourselves. The college student leaving her significant other for adventures abroad must reframe her identity. She's not Joe's girl anymore—she is a woman traveling on her own. The new widow must rediscover who she is after so many years of being one of a couple. If she decides to move to an assisted living facility, she has to discover who she is in this unfamiliar place, faced every time she opens her door with the unalterable fact that she is elderly. Her children, grieving the death of their father, realize that they have moved from being their mother's children to taking care of her. All of these changes entail a new self-image, a new sense of who one is.

The second task of grieving is to internalize what was lost, so that it remains present in our lives, but in a new way. As the widow's grown children help sell her home, they must learn to think of the home they grew up in not as "a place I can return to" but as "a place I can visit in my imagination." Perhaps they can use their memories of that home to help them relax in times of stress. The widow will be doing the same thing in relationship to her husband. He's no longer physically available to her, but she will have her memories. She might find herself, in her imagination, asking her beloved how he would handle a situation or telling him when important things happen. She might even experience times when she feels wrapped in his love.

The Journey of Grief. Grieving is a journey. And although not everyone's path through the process is the same, there is a general path that many of us follow. We move out of the flatlands of "life as usual" through two landscapes before returning to the changed life that awaits us.

The first landscape is the gray tunnel of shock. When the loss is devastating, our minds often send us straight into denial. It's a kindly move, giving us time to adjust to a loss. Driving to the hospital after being notified of a son's bad accident, parents finds themselves thinking that this is "just a dream" that they'll wake up from. This reaction is normal and healthy.

When denial ends, we experience shock. The mind withdraws all energy from nonessential activities to focus on coping with loss. People in shock experience life as if through a fog. They are on autopilot. They use words like "stunned" and "numb" to describe their feelings. They can't focus to drive, they don't want to eat, and they often need help making decisions.

We move through the landscape of acute shock at our own pace: some in minutes, others in days. But eventually the fog clears for a while, the numbness eases, and we start to get a glimpse of the next landscape.

The second landscape of grief is a bleak mountain range: all jagged peaks, impossible climbs, frightening heights, and hard, hard work. Many times people who are bereaved for the first time in their lives will say, on first glimpse of this landscape, that they will not be able to master its tasks. And in subsequent bereavements they will say, "I know I have done this before, but I have no idea how I did it." This is a big mountain, and climbing it may take months or even years. Of course, what we all want to do is move from shock directly to the green pastures of "normal" on the other side of this mountain, but it doesn't work that way.

During this unwelcome journey, we feel sadness—sometimes acute, sometimes a dull pain accompanying every step taken. Every reminder of the loss brings a fresh wave of grief. Sometimes the sadness becomes emptiness or even despair. Not every moment is equally difficult. There are times when the path flattens out for a while and the work eases—but then a holiday hits, or an anniversary, or another small loss, and it's an uphill slog over the rocks again.

Dealing with Anger. Sufferers and those around them are often surprised by how anger can bubble up on this journey of grief. People find themselves angry at those who seem to have caused the loss. They are angry at the rough features of the terrible landscape they find themselves in. They are angry at those around them who don't seem to care or who have attempted to comfort them with a clumsy word. They may be angry at themselves for not being able to prevent the loss or for all the flaws in the relationship. They are often angry at God, whether they believe in God or not. Above all, they are angry at the person they have lost, who has seemingly abandoned them.

People who are grieving often feel guilty for being angry. But anger, like denial, is a normal and healthy part of the grieving process. It will pass faster if we can simply acknowledge what we are feeling.

Making It Through. The goal of the journey through grief is to find a new normal on the other side of the mountain. Most people are vastly relieved to discover that they are not alone on this mountain, that other sufferers are toiling away. This is the time when bereavement support groups can be very helpful. These groups offer the company of those who understand the landscape of grief and who are not impatient with the length of the journey.

After some months, the path starts to get easier. We start to notice the lovely views and take some interest in the people around us. In our spiritual imagination, we might see that we have had some help on this journey, that we've been carried along in some mysterious but comforting way. We start to develop a new self-image as a person who has coped with this loss. We begin to realize that the person or thing we lost is still with us, but in a different way.

At some point, we may declare ourselves to have healed. But even then, a holiday, the sight of something just like what we lost, or a whiff of a smell transports us back to our loss. Those visits actually start to take on a sweetness, even in their difficulty, because a part of us is glad to be reminded of what was once so important to us. When that happens, we know our journey of grieving is nearly complete.

Activities

Before the gathering, reflect on loss and grief by doing one or more of the following activities.

Practice Letting Go. Letting go is one of the major tasks on the mountain of grief and the best way to prepare ourselves for large losses is to attend to the small ones throughout our lives. Take notice of the losses you are experiencing in your life right now. From changing relationships to our ever-changing bodies, we always have many losses hovering around us. Often all we need to do to put these losses to rest is to notice and honor them. Make a list of your losses and process them in some way—write in your journal, talk to a friend about them, or simply be gently aware of your need to let go. Each day can be an opportunity to let go of something, and every goodbye you say is a practice for the big goodbyes.

Honor a Memory. Honoring the memory of someone or something you have lost can help you work through grief. For example, some find it helpful to plant a memorial tree or create a scrapbook to preserve memories. Some ease their grief by giving compassionate help to others, such as by volunteering in a hospital or nursing home. One person found relief through joining a group of friends hiking weekly. Think about ways you have honored, or could honor, someone or something you have lost. Take some time in the next few days or weeks to honor a memory in a way that is meaningful to you.

Remember Through Music. For some, music can touch us in unique ways. It can help us move through the years and cherish times or persons lost. For instance, a certain part of the Brahms Requiem might help someone feel close to her mother, who has been dead for many years. Play or listen to music that is dear to you because it takes you back to special times and special people in your life.

Journaling Suggestions. List the losses that have been hard for you. Whom have you lost to death? What relationships have you lost to breakups, moving away, or drifting apart? Have you ever experienced a major loss of material goods in a fire, theft, or divorce? How about pets? What about the loss of a role, as when graduating, leaving a job, or facing an "empty nest"? Have you ever lost a part of your body or some of your abilities? What other losses stand out for you?

Throughout our lives, we bump up against the task of giving up a former self-image. Write about some of those times for you.

Times of acute grief are often times of openness to the spiritual side of life. If this has ever happened to you, write about it.

Some people who have lost a loved one put their grief to use by working to prevent others from suffering a similar loss. If this is true for you, what did you do and how was the experience? If you have not experienced this, reflect on how you think it might be for you.

Review your lists of losses (see Journaling Suggestions above). Think about a loss, past or present, that you are willing to share with the group.

GATHERING

Candle Lighting

This is the light of faith and hope and love, which shines in our lives even in the darkest times. This is the light of the gathered community, which holds us and comforts us when we grieve. This is the light of our ongoing search for truth and meaning, which gives a path even through loss. We light this light and invoke the light that illumines life and death and shines beyond both.

—Christine Robinson

On Our Hearts   10 minutes

Silence   3 minutes

Shared Readings

We are not accustomed to thinking of grief in any way other than that associated with death. Nevertheless, people grieve when they clearly cease to have the protections of childhood. They grieve when they go away from home for the first time. They grieve when they have to give up their first love. They grieve when they suffer a serious illness or injury. They grieve when they leave each stage of life for another. People grieve when they change jobs or homes; when they leave one beloved and comfortable community for another. For a teenager the end of an infatuation or friendship can bring on a grief as profound and as serious as the grief which may follow the death of a grandparent.

—John Nichols

It doesn't interest me how old you are . . . I want to know if you have touched the center of your own sorrow, if you have been opened by life's betrayals or have become shriveled and closed from fear of further pain! I want to know if you can sit with pain, mine or your own, without moving to hide it or fade it or fix it. . . . It doesn't interest me to know where you live or how much money you have. I want to know if you can get up after the night of grief and despair, weary and bruised to the bone, and do what needs to be done for the children.

—Oriah Mountain Dreamer

It's possible I am pushing through solid rock
in flintlike layers, as the ore lies, alone;
I am such a long way in I see no way through,
and no space: everything is close to my face,
and everything close to my face is stone.

I don't have much knowledge yet in grief—
so this massive darkness makes me small.
You be the master: make yourself fierce, break in:
then your great transforming will happen to me,
and my great grief cry will happen to you.

—Rainer Maria Rilke

He was my North, my South, my East and West,
My working week and my Sunday rest,
My noon, my midnight, my talk, my song;
I thought that love would last for ever: I was wrong.

—W. H. Auden

Sharing   60 minutes

Closing Activity

Naming Our Losses

Closing Words

In the rising of the sun and its going down,

We remember them.

In the blowing of the wind and in the chill of winter,

We remember them.

In the opening buds and in the rebirth of spring,

We remember them.

In the blueness of the sky and in the warmth of summer,

We remember them.

In the rustling of leaves and in the beauty of autumn,

We remember them.

In the beginning of the year and when it ends,

We remember them.

When we are weary and in need of strength,

We remember them.

When we are lost and are sick of heart,

We remember them.

When we have joys we yearn to share,

We remember them.

So long as we live, they too shall live,

For they are now a part of us,

As we remember them.

—Sylvan Kamens and Jack Riemer

Conclude the gathering by singing "Thank You for Your Loving Hands" (page xii) and making any necessary announcements.

Money

∾

BEFORE YOU GATHER

Money is power, freedom, a cushion, the root of all evil, the sum of blessings.
   —Carl Sandburg

Sorting out the place of money in your life is the soul's work.
   —Stephen Jenkinson

For where your treasure is, there your heart will be also.
   —Matthew 6:21

Money often costs too much.
   —Ralph Waldo Emerson

Who is wise? He that learns from everyone. Who is powerful? He that governs his passions. Who is rich? He that is content. Who is that? Nobody.
   —Ben Franklin

It's not what you earn, it's what you spend.
   —Paul Clitheroe

Consider This

"Your money or your life," says the outlaw in the old joke. When there is no answer, he prods the rich man with his gun and yells, "Your money or your life! Are you deaf?" "No!" cries the rich man. "I just can't decide!"

The odd thing about money is that it *is* our lives in such deep ways. Our money represents the fruits of our labors, the years of our lives we have spent at work, the value others have placed on our efforts. If we have inherited money, that money represents a gift of the self of another person, their labor and creativity. Money is shorthand for time and talent, and our time and our talents are who we deeply are. Money plays an important part in the comforts we have in our lives and the security we enjoy about the future. We pursue happiness, in part, with money. For all that we intuit that the love of money can be the root of all evil, we want it. "I've been rich and I've been poor," said Mae West, "and rich is better."

Money is our life in a deep way, but it's not our only life. Having money is better than not having money only if the acquisition of that money has not eclipsed other important values, like family, creativity, spiritual life, and friendships. Acquiring riches often separates a person from family and friends, if only because it takes time and focus. It's easy to develop a suspicious attitude toward one's neighbors when one has considerably more material wealth than they do. Sometimes the wealthy ask themselves, "Do they really love me, or do they just love my money?" Further, the acquisition of money has an addictive potential. The desire for money can overcome love, common sense, health, and all the other values that make life good. In the end, of course, money cannot buy us health, friendship, family, or even security, helpful as it can be in all of these areas.

Poverty is just as injurious to the whole of our life as addiction to wealth. Real poverty, like wealth, can separate one from one's fellows. Poverty can keep people from being creative or furthering their educational or spiritual goals. It can thrust a person into a frantic and single-minded focus on earning money or using dubious means to earn money. Sometimes monastics of various faiths practice poverty as a spiritual discipline. However, this would better be called simplicity, since these persons, even if they own very little, usually have enough security as a group to keep the damages of true poverty at bay. Real poverty is rarely good for the spirit. Great wealth is dangerous to the spirit. Between poverty and wealth is a point of balance for every person—that point of "just enough."

Wealth and Riches. In pursuit of a balanced attitude toward money, perhaps our goal in life should be to live richly rather than to be wealthy. Here's the distinction.

"Wealthy" is a social lifestyle of those who have the most in a society, whether that's the one woman in the village who has a goat and a few chickens or the multibillionaire of our society. "Wealthy" is not measured in any way except by comparison with others. That's one reason the pursuit of wealth is addictive. It is a nebulous goal. The grass is always greener somewhere else, and one never can quite say, "I've achieved wealth and can now turn to other things."

"Rich" is a broader and deeper word than "wealthy." You can be rich with friends or enjoy something richly. A color is rich if it is deep and well pigmented. A rich dessert has a certain depth and complexity of taste that a Popsicle or donut just doesn't have. In music, a rich tone is one that has a full range of overtones just under the surface. Thoreau believed he was rich because he knew the trees and animals around his hut at Walden Pond.

Most of us will never be wealthy, but many of us could be rich. Being rich involves having enough money to meet our needs without worry and living a life that involves many values and pleasures.

Having enough is a two-sided prescription. It means both that one has income and that one's wants do not exceed that income. To become rich, one can either find a large source of income or one contain one's desires and enjoy life as it is. Thoreau said, "A man is rich in proportion to the number of things which he can afford to let alone." Lao Tzu came to this by another route: "He who is contented is rich."

When our pleasures have depth, it is much easier to be content with fewer of them. Like the rich dessert that satisfies in just a few bites, deep pleasures keep on giving. Cultivating deep pleasures helps us keep our wants small enough that our income becomes "enough." One trip abroad with a dear friend can be enjoyed for years of anticipating and remembering. Money given to a grand project of some kind brings the quiet pleasures of generosity long after purchased baubles would have faded. Using our life's energy to provide for ourselves and our families is deeply satisfying. These are all good things.

Balancing Life and Money. There are basically three things we do with money: share it, save it, and spend it. It is good to be intentional about what these proportions will be and disciplined about carrying them out. The biblical tithe (10 percent) is a standard of sharing that many people adopt. We should be saving at least that much; in some periods of our life we should be saving more. If we cannot do these things, our spending is out of balance. We are encouraged in this society to spend as a cure for all that troubles us, but this is a false road. Overspending is an out-of-balance reaction to an out-of-balance life.

On the other side, if earning money has begun to take up so much of our life that our friends, family, and hobbies must be put aside; if we hate going to work; if work is making us ill or forcing us to go against our values; then we have to make some serious decisions. Money is an important part of life, but it is not the whole of it. When the whole is seriously suffering, it may be time to simplify our desires and make some changes so that the whole of our life can be in balance.

Your money or your life? Let's strive to keep both—in balance.

Activities

Before the gathering, reflect on money by doing one or more of the following activities.

Checkbook Theology. Look through your checkbook register or credit card bills. If you had just arrived from Mars and were given these documents as representative of the values of an Earthling, what would you conclude about their owner? What does he or she care about?

Planned Giving. If you were given ten thousand dollars with the instructions that you had to give it away (but not to your family), to whom would you give the money? Make a table listing the groups or persons you would give money to, what you would want the money to be used for, and the percentages or amounts of money dispersed to each group or person.

Journaling Suggestions. Think about the last few times you spent money on luxuries or "frills." What motivated that spending? How did you feel?

Think about the last few times you gave money away. Why did you do it? How did you feel?

What do you want to do that you can't do because you don't have enough money?

Describe what "living richly" might mean for you.

Describe how money is one or more of the following things in your life: power, freedom, a cushion, the root of all evil, the sum of blessings.

What did money represent in your family when you were growing up, and what were you taught about its use? What was the most important message your parents sent to you about money? What is your most significant memory about money?

Think about the percentage of your income you share, save, and spend. Are you satisfied with the balance between these uses? What other choices would you consider making?

Bring a big handful of coins to the group meeting. Think about the feelings the topic of money brings up for you now and how it was viewed by your family when you were a child. Give some thought to what you are willing to share with the group.

∾

GATHERING

Candle Lighting

We gather this hour as people of faith
With joys and sorrows, gifts and needs.
We light this beacon of hope,
sign of our quest
for truth and meaning,
in celebration of the life we share together.
  —Christine Robinson

On Our Hearts 10 minutes

Silence 3 minutes

Shared Readings

Look at your attitude and behavior regarding money and ask your-self, "Are behavior and attitude in line with the values I attempt to live by?" Our frustrations around money are often due to our behavior being out of sync with our values. That's when we find that our money is in control of us instead of us being in control of our money.
  —Davis Fisher

Money is a paradox in our culture—it enslaves, yet it also frees; it is intensely private, but it is also very public; it measures worth, yet it is no measure of real worth; it destroys yet also creates.
—Victoria Curtiss

I am surrounded by those who put their trust
    in possessions and money
I am not taken in.
What is precious in life can't be had in the marketplace
What is important about us is not what we acquire,
    but what we do to add love, goodness, and
    beauty to the world.
It's the size of our hearts, not the size of our houses,
It's our wisdom, not our fame.
—Psalm 49, adapted by Christine Robinson

Sharing   60 minutes

Closing Activity

Spending Coins

Closing Words

Respect the life energy you are putting into your job. Money is simply something you trade your life energy for. Trade it with purpose and integrity for increased earnings. Ask yourself: Am I making a living or making a dying?
—Joe Dominguez and Vicki Robin

Conclude the gathering by singing "Thank You for Your Loving Hands" (page xii) and making any necessary announcements.

Nature

∾

BEFORE YOU GATHER

It seems as if the day was not wholly profane, in which we have given heed to some natural object.
—Henry David Thoreau

The world is holy. We are holy. All life is holy. Daily prayers are delivered on the lips of breaking waves, the whisperings of grasses, the shimmering of leaves.
—Terry Tempest Williams

Fierce landscapes remind us that what we long for and what we fear most are both already within us.
—Belden Lane

Tell me the landscape in which you live, and I will tell you who you are.
—José Ortega y Gasset

Consider This

Nature, whether oceans, deserts, mountains, rosebushes, pets, or trout streams, offers us several avenues to experiences of spirit. This experience of transcendence in nature is the foundation of Pagan and earth-centered faiths, but it is also found in the Christian world, from Saint Francis to the newest of the creation-centered spiritualities. Nature-inspired spirituality was one hallmark of the nineteenth-century American thinkers known as the Transcendentalists. Henry David Thoreau stated in his journal, "My profession is to be always on the alert to find God in nature, to know his lurking-places, to attend all the oratorios, the operas, in nature." Even persons who do not have traditional beliefs about God and those who do not easily experience the divine in meditation, scripture, speaking in tongues, and so on often have profound experiences in nature. Whatever our theology, whatever our language of reverence, Nature has gifts for our spiritual lives.

Oneness. The first of nature's gifts to the soul is the experience of oneness. When we sit by a stream, gaze at the clouds, stroke a pet, or look out through the trees during a mountain hike, one thing that we might experience—especially if we are expecting or hoping for it—is a sense of unity with the universe. Even a whiff of a neighbor's flowers on a twilight walk can bring that wonderful, mystical feeling: "I am right here. I belong." People who enjoy hunting and fishing sometimes say that one of the attractions is the excuse to get out "where there's only you and the morning" (and if pressed, they might say that the distinction between themselves and the morning feels blurred). Many skiers make a similar claim about their sport. "I'm at one with the mountain," they say, and they know that this is a valuable, spiritual experience. Experiencing the sacred in nature is a practice deeply rooted in American spiritual tradition.

The Transcendentalists spoke repeatedly of their own experiences of oneness in nature. In his essay *Nature*, Ralph Waldo Emerson describes such a moment. "Standing on the bare ground—my head bathed by the blithe air, and uplifted into infinite space—all mean egotism vanishes. I become a transparent eyeball; I am nothing; I see all; the currents of the Universal Being circulate through me; I am part or particle of God."

If you are one of the many people who most reliably experience that expansive sense of unity out in nature, then regular excursions to gardens, parks, mountains, riversides, and oceans should be a part of the way you care for your soul.

Humility. Nature reminds us that we are small and that our lives are surrounded in mystery. This deeply spiritual feeling, sometimes called humility, can be found by being in a little boat on a big sea, or looking out on grand vistas, or spending the night in a sleeping bag under the stars. Humility is a sobering and necessary corrective to the heady discovery that we are at one with the universe.

Some people dislike the word *humility*, because it has connotations of bowing and scraping before an arrogant power. But the root of the world humility is the same as the root of words like *humus*, meaning fertile topsoil or earth, and human. Humility has connotations of groundedness and of connection to earth and humanity. The truth of the matter is that we are specks of life and consciousness in immensity; short lived, soft shelled, vulnerable.

Our smallness and vulnerability is a countercultural truth— not one that we're likely to dwell on in our workaday lives. Our factories, hospitals, and shopping malls operate on opposite assumptions: that we know most of what we need to know and are in control of most of the things we ought to control. Experiences in nature offer a healthy corrective to this hubris.

Mindfulness. Nature also offers us a variety of opportunities to be mindful—to practice that combination of relaxation and alertness that is the meditative state, and to be appreciative of the gifts of life.

In almost all excursions into nature, we have to pare down, take only what's necessary, enjoy—really enjoy—tepid water and real sweat and sometimes even real danger. We are inclined to slow down and appreciate. The sandwich we would have devoured without thinking in the kitchen is good to the last crumb when fished out of a backpack at the top of the trail. The ants that would have been an occasion for the bug spray if they'd been in the dining room become an object of fascination as we eat at a picnic. The moon that we barely notice in town is a crystal beauty when we stare at it from our campsite in the woods.

A special subset of mindfulness is found in the taking of risks that require a focus and intense awareness that most of us don't cultivate in our daily lives, unless we are practiced at meditating. Activities like fly fishing and mountain climbing offer us this gift. When hanging by a rope on the face of a cliff, we're really present, not worrying about our job or wondering how to fix the house. All of our attention is on the cliff, the day, and the task. Taking risks, or what some part of our brain perceives as risks (no matter that the guide has never lost a raft, that the mule has never stumbled, that the rope has been carefully inspected), fills our bodies with those "fight or flight" hormones and then actually gives us a way to use them up, giving us a natural high at the end of it all.

The gifts of time spent in nature—a sense of oneness, an appropriate humility, and opportunities for mindfulness and focus— combine to give us a realistic and holistic sense of our place in things. That experience of realness and truth is precious and deeply spiritual. Nature's beauty and grandeur are potent aides to our spiritual lives.

Activities

Before the gathering, reflect on nature by doing one or more of the following activities.

Notice the Season. Get yourself out of the house or apartment at daybreak, sundown, or both, and experience what is happening to the earth. Notice where the sun is in the sky. How long is the day? What signs of the season are present? Are plants resting, growing vigorously, or dropping leaves? Do you really feel the heat, the cold, the wind? Try to find a comfortable way to spend some time just sitting or walking and noticing the season.

Practice Mindfulness in Nature. If you have a meditation practice, try either meditating outdoors or using a natural object as your focus. If you don't have a meditation practice, just try sitting and gazing at the stars, a part of the garden, a tree, or even a pet or houseplant. Notice details. Appreciate.

Bring Nature Indoors. In our gardens and indoor spaces, we often cultivate bits of nature to remind us of our experiences in the natural world. Plants, pets, fountains, nature-inspired color choices, and pictures of outdoor scenes can enhance our spiritual life. Bring the outdoors into your living space to remind yourself of nature's beauty and grandeur.

Journaling Suggestions. Most people can tell a story of a time when they felt "opened" or awestruck by something in nature. Alternatively, many of us can remember when an experience in nature lulled us into a deep sense of peace. Or we have felt at one with the universe while in nature. Write about your memories of some profound experiences in nature.

Terry Tempest Williams, an author and naturalist, speaks of breaking waves and whispering grasses as nature's prayers. Where in your life do you notice the prayers of nature?

What landscape do you live in (or visit often)? How does that make you who you are?

How have you reacted when you have discovered some way in which nature has been harmed?

Think about the experiences you've had in nature this week and in the past. Choose one you are willing to talk about at the gathering. Decide which of the four elements of the Pagan tradition—earth, air, fire, or water—your experience embodies. For instance, you might choose fire if you've found yourself drawn to stargazing this week, or water if you want to tell about an experience you had at the ocean. Bring an item that is symbolic of the element you have chosen to the gathering. You

could bring a candle to symbolize fire, a feather or a balloon for air, a
rock for earth, a shell for water, or anything else that works for you.

∾

GATHERING

Candle Lighting

All are but parts of one stupendous whole,
Whose body Nature is, and God the soul.
  —Alexander Pope

On Our Hearts   10 minutes

Silence   3 minutes

Shared Readings

If I spent enough time with the tiniest of creatures, even a caterpil-
lar, I would never have to prepare a sermon, so full of God is every
creature.
  —Meister Eckhart

It is our quiet time.
We do not speak, because the voices are within us.
It is our quiet time.
We do not walk, because the earth is all within us.
It is our quiet time.
We do not dance, because the music has lifted us to a place where
    the spirit is.

It is our quiet time.
We rest with all of nature. We wake when the seven sisters wake.
We greet them in the sky over the opening of the kiva.
    —Nancy Wood

Sharing   60 minutes

Closing Activity

Taking Elements Home

Closing Words

We stand in awe of an infinity
which we cannot begin to comprehend.
We set ourselves to live in tune with the universe—
that we may be glad with the gladness of people of faith.

Yes, time and time again we have gone astray,
We have despoiled this beautiful, wonderful world
And dealt unjustly with our companions on the planet.
The law of love is a hard law.
In our prayer and then in our lives,
we return to the Way.
    —Psalm 106, adapted by Christine Robinson

*Conclude the gathering by singing "Thank You for Your Loving Hands"
(page xii) and making any necessary announcements.*

Success and Failure

∾

BEFORE YOU GATHER

If you don't accept failure as a possibility, you don't set high goals, you don't branch out, you don't try—you don't take the risk.
—Rosalynn Carter

Man has places in his heart which do not yet exist, and into them enters suffering in order that they may have existence.
—Leon Bloy

Do not believe that he who seeks to comfort you now lives untroubled among the simple and quiet words that sometimes do you good. His life has much difficulty and sadness and remains far behind yours. Were it otherwise he would never have been able to find those words.
—Rainer Maria Rilke

Grace enters into our experience precisely at this point where we are wounded, where our longings are deepest and most inarticulate.
—Alan Jones

Consider This

Success almost always feels good and failure almost always feels bad, but in the totality of our lives, things are usually more complicated. No doubt all of us can think of times in our own lives or the lives of friends when success led to tragedy or when what we first experienced as "failure" was a blessing in disguise. Perhaps we can remember times when we succeeded at the wrong goals or when, looking back, it was clear that the cost of success was too high. Nonetheless, most of us feel driven to pursue success and avoid failure, and the lack of the former and the weight of the latter are often major elements of dissatisfaction in our lives.

Society gives us broad guidelines about success and failure: success as a certain kind of lifestyle, being unemployed as failure, and so on. Our parents and families give us narrower guidelines about success: what kind of degree we are "supposed" to have or what kind of spouse is acceptable. While those definitions may haunt us, in the end, we must each define success for ourselves. "I know you want me to go to college, Mom," a teen might say, "but I feel drawn to woodworking, and I'm going to trade school to learn that skill. Going to college is *your* definition of success. My definition of success is to become skilled at a craft."

It's a harder job to define our own failures, but we have to do that too. The woman who was taught that a single or childless woman has failed at life's important tasks must rewrite that script if she is to be free to choose to be single or to focus on her career. Even those who have just experienced something they define as a failure—being fired, for instance—have to in the end say to themselves, "I may have failed at that, but I learned from it, and I am not a failure as a person."

The Whole of Life. Our lives will have both success and failure in them, and both are best dealt with by widening our horizons. Success can be dangerous if it causes us to concentrate on developing one aspect of ourselves to the detriment of all others. We've all known successful people who were lured by their talents, luck, and hard work into a terribly one-sided life. The business tycoon whose only real relationship with his family is through the paycheck he provides them is the classic example. We've all seen the opposite, too: the devoted mom who suddenly realizes that all she can do is nurture others. We all worry about child actors and musical prodigies: Will their success ruin them as people? Will it rob them of the childhood they need to develop all of their talents? Will they hate their parents for pushing them in only one direction?

We worry about children because we know how important it is for them to grow in many directions. But it's just as important for all of us. When life brings us success, we need to make sure that we're also healthy and balanced. In the end, our great success is going to seem hollow if we miss our children's childhood, or if we become so specialized that we can't be flexible in our market any more. In the end, we all need variety in our lives.

This diversification serves us well when we feel we are failing or have failed. While we do what needs to be done to solve the problem and learn from it, we can shore up our self-esteem by broadening our activities. If your teenager is being impossible, you do what a good parent must do, but it might also be time to take those painting lessons. If there's been a business downturn and you're worried about being laid off, you do what you can to prepare for that and then turn to an exercise program that will give you a sense of accomplishment. When the inevitable failures come along, we need to invest in the parts of our lives that are successful.

The Widest View. In both success and failure, the task is to learn to see yourself as an all-knowing God might see you: a unique, precious person to the core of your being, completely aside from what you do that succeeds and fails by worldly standards. Sometimes we speak of knowing ourselves as loved by God or a child of God. Some speak of the worth and dignity of every individual or the core of light within each person. All these phrases attempt to remind us that our essence of being is more important than our successes and failures. It might very well be that you've failed at something, perhaps something very important. Perhaps you look back after a divorce and really see the part you played in the demise of your marriage. Maybe you lost your job for a good reason. Perhaps your failure was caused by inattentiveness or pride or addictions. Those are all matters of your doing, not your being.

Seeing into our hearts as that all-knowing God might see us keeps us balanced in times of success, too. We know, if we're honest with ourselves, how much of our success was luck, inborn talent, and being in the right place at the right time. We know, if we will look at ourselves whole, that our health and our families were as much a part of our success as hard work and winning ways. If we stay aware of these things in our success, we will avoid the swollen head that is so difficult to live with and so often contributes to eventual failure.

If you don't like all this God talk, the philosopher Spinoza coined a phrase that conveys the same idea. He spoke of the importance of being able to see things *sub specie aeternitatis*: "under the aspect of eternity." When we cultivate the ability to see ourselves in this infinitely large light, our daily successes and failures won't throw us. Under the aspect of eternity, I know myself as a basically, but not completely, good person who makes mistakes and does not always live up to my ideals, but who continues to work at them. Under the aspect of eternity, I know myself as one whose success is built on a foundation for which I can be thankful but not self-righteous. Under the aspect of eternity, I know myself whole, failures and successes together.

Our lives are filled with successes and failures large and small, insignificant and devastating, triumphant and terrible. The question is never whether we will experience successes and failures, but how we will deal with them when we do. Will they, in the end, contribute to or detract from the growth of our souls?

When we take care to define success and failure for ourselves, when we keep a broad agenda in life, and when we learn to see ourselves as ultimately lovable and worthy to our very core, the successes of our lives will enrich us rather than endanger us, and our failures will hurt us but not destroy us.

Activities

Before the gathering, reflect on success and failure by doing one or more of the following activities.

The Gift of Failure. Rachel Naomi Remen, a physician and author, tells the story of a cancer patient who drew a picture of a vase with deep black cracks, the image of his broken body. Several years later, he looked at this picture and said, "Oh, this one isn't finished." He took a yellow crayon and began to draw lines radiating from the crack. "You see, here—where it is broken—this is where the light comes through." We can grow strong at the broken places. To connect this with your life, draw a vase (with a shape that has meaning for you) and mark it with the cracks that symbolize various failures. Label the cracks. How much light (learning and growth) shines through each?

Ask Someone Else. Perhaps there is a success or failure that particularly puzzles you. Were others involved? Could you ask them about their experience of that situation and your role in it? Sometimes it is easier to initiate difficult conversations when we have an assignment to do so and can ask someone to help us complete it. In that case, you've got your assignment.

Journaling Suggestions. Thinking back to your childhood, what messages did you get about success and failure from your family, teachers, and peers?

How do you define success and failure at this point in your life?

Considering your adult life, what would you list as your most important successes and failures? How have they contributed to your growth?

If you have you had successes that backfired or failures that turned out to be blessings, journal about these occasions.

In different phases of life, we focus on different things. What's your focus now? How might you broaden that focus with new interests, hobbies, exercise, or spirituality?

It is often easiest to see the pure essence or inner beauty of an infant or child, harder to see it in adults, and hardest of all to see it in yourself. When are you most in touch with your essence? When can you see yourself "under the aspect of eternity"?

Think about what successes or failures you are willing to share with the group. As you did the activities this week, did you find yourself focused on a particular episode of success or failure in your life?

∾

GATHERING

Candle Lighting

For every time we make a mistake and we decide to start again:
We light this candle.
For every time we are lonely and we let someone be our friend:
We light this candle.
For every time we are disappointed and we choose to hope:
We light this candle.
　—M. Maureen Killoran

On Our Hearts　　10 minutes

Silence　　3 minutes

Shared Readings

To laugh often and much, to win the respect of intelligent people and the affection of children, to earn the appreciation of honest critics and endure the betrayal of false friends, to appreciate beauty, to find the best in others, to leave the world a bit better, whether by a healthy child, a garden patch, or a redeemed social condition; to know even one life has breathed easier because you have lived. This is to have succeeded.
—Bessie Anderson Stanley

I am not I. I am this one
Walking beside me whom I do not see,
Whom at times I manage to visit.
And whom at other times I forget;
Who remains calm and silent while I talk,
And forgives, gently, when I hate,
Who walks where I am not,
Who will remain standing when I die.
—Juan Ramón Jiménez, translated by Robert Bly

Instead of showing ourselves as we truly are, we show ourselves as we believe others want us to be. We wear masks, and with practice we do it better and better, and they serve us well—except that it gets very lonely inside the mask, because inside the mask that each of us wears there is a person who both longs to be known and fears to be known.
—Frederick Buechner

It is not the critic who counts: not the man who points out how the strong man stumbles or where the doer of deeds could have done better. The credit belongs to the man who is actually in the arena, whose face is marred by dust and sweat and blood, who strives valiantly, who errs and comes up short again and again, because there is no effort without error or shortcoming, but who knows the great enthusiasms, the great devotions, who spends himself for a worthy cause; who, at the best, knows, in the end, the triumph of high achievement, and who, at the worst, if he fails, at least he fails while daring greatly, so that his place shall never be with those cold and timid souls who knew neither victory nor defeat.

—Theodore Roosevelt

Sharing   60 minutes

Closing Activity

Paper Stars

Closing Words

O Star (the fairest one in sight), . . .
It asks a little of us here.
It asks of us a certain height,
So when at times the mob is swayed
To carry praise or blame too far,
We may take something like a star
To stay our minds on and be staid.

—Robert Frost

Conclude the gathering by singing "Thank You for Your Loving Hands" (page xii) and making any necessary announcements.

Friendship

∾

BEFORE YOU GATHER

Remember no man is a failure who has friends.
  —*It's a Wonderful Life*

I get glimpses of myself in other people's eyes. I try to be careful
whom I use as a mirror: my husband; my children; my mother; the
friends of my right hand.
  —Madeleine L'Engle

Those truly linked don't need correspondence. When they meet
again after many years apart, their friendship is as true as ever.
  —Deng Ming-Dao

Let there be spaces in your togetherness,
And let the winds of the heavens dance between you.
Love one another, but make not a bond of love.
  —Kahlil Gibran

Consider This

A friend is one with whom you share your soul—your innermost
being. That means that the best lovers are also friends, that young
children often have their parents as friends, and in the best of all

worlds, grown children and parents share a friendship. It also means that friendships can be sudden and short-lived as we come and go through each other's lives, and that even people who live together for years may not be especially close friends.

This definition of friendship excludes many important, pleasant, and useful relationships that we tend to call friendships, but which don't involve much deep sharing. We can eat lunch and talk politics and recipes with the same folks for years and never really know them. We may trust our neighbor with our spare key, but not with the depths of ourselves. With friends, we take the risk of knowing and being known. We continue to get closer to them even though we know that there will be loss in our future. And in spite of the temptation to make them "just like us," we give them space to be who they uniquely are.

Comfort and Risk. There's nothing quite as wonderful as sharing something important with another person and feeling known and accepted in return. But there's a risk in friendship. Because we've let that person in behind our defenses, shared our secrets, and asked for acceptance, no one can hurt us like a friend. The deeper the relationship, the greater the potential that a slip of the tongue can sting, that thoughtless action will wound, that we will feel rejected, taken for granted, or used. "But I thought we were friends," we mourn, most often to ourselves, over these bruises of relationship, these slights and slips that we'd think nothing of had they come from just a neighbor or coworker. When it comes from a friend, it hurts.

But when it comes from a friend, the relationship means enough to patch it up, forgive, and go on. That means hearing the other person's side, forgiving each other's foolishness, understanding one another's lives. These understandings enlarge our souls. They help us learn to forgive our own foolishness and be sympathetic to our own missteps. Our friends give us our greatest hurts, and we give our greatest hurts to our friends. The hurts themselves become the fuel for greater friendship as we learn to understand each other and ourselves, accept our flaws and foibles, and become more aware of who we are.

Love and Loss. Every time we make a friend, we experience the joy of knowing and being known, and put ourselves in line for the experience of loss. At the same time, the fact that we won't have each other around forever makes us want to open up to each other and gives us the impetus to do it now. That is one reason why we so often cherish memories of friendships made at camps, retreats, and professional conferences. Knowing that the week or the weekend will soon be over, we take risks that we'd never take on home territory.

The mystery goes deeper. The practice our friendships give us in saying goodbye prepares us for the final goodbyes that happen in our dying. While having rich friendships may make it all the more difficult to let go of our lives, those who have had satisfying, meaningful lives do seem to find a sense of peace in the end, while whose who have not known or given love are more apt to despair. Love and loss are twined in and through our living and our struggles. Both love and loss make our lives full. The sheer joy of knowing others, and being known and accepted in ourselves, keeps us taking the risks of friendship in the face of the real pain of loss.

Unity and Boundaries. The Roman poet Cicero called a friend a "second self," and Aristotle said that friendship is "a single soul dwelling in two bodies." We moderns believe, with good reason, that friendship also requires boundaries. The fact of the matter is that there are two souls and two selves. Each must have its integrity or there can be no friendship, only mush.

The irony is that we can only be close because we are separate. If we are not absolutely sure of our separateness, we can never risk closeness, even momentarily. What makes our friendships valuable to us is that we can be who we most truly are and experience others as they truly are. We must resist the temptation to make our friends in our own image or to become so enamored of them that we are no longer ourselves.

Friendship thrives when we honor others' boundaries. This is especially important and difficult when we are friends for the long term—partners, siblings, parents, and children. There must always be spaces in our togetherness to let the other grow in his or her own way. We must ask the same space and permission of those who love us.

A spouse enters therapy, begins a new career, or finds a passion for art or politics or spiritual life. Is the other spouse scared? Of course. Does she clutch? We advise her not to. We tell her to breathe through her anxieties, work on her own growth, and show a befriending, but not controlling, interest in the intimate stranger who is emerging. This is not easy. But from the spaces in their togetherness, their relationship grows and enriches both. That's the great benefit of friendship.

Activities

Before the gathering, reflect on friendship by doing one or more of the following activities.

Friendship Haiku. Write a haiku to tell a friend how much he or she means to you. A haiku is a kind of Japanese poetry that has three lines. The first line has five syllables, the second line has seven syllables, and the last line has five syllables. It doesn't rhyme, and there is often much left out—phrases that may be connected or pondered in the reader's mind. For instance:

Connections growing
Budding stems between our hearts
Riotous blooming

A Scripture of Love. Many call the verses below one of the best definitions of love. Spend some time with this great passage—perhaps even take a line a day, ponder it, and write about it in your journal. What part of your life does each line touch?

If I speak in the tongues of mortals and of angels, but do not have love, I am a noisy gong or a clanging cymbal. And if I have prophetic powers, and understand all mysteries and all knowledge, and if I have all faith, so as to remove mountains, but do not have love, I am nothing. If I give away all my possessions, and if I hand over my body so that I may boast, but do not have love, I gain nothing.

Love is patient; love is kind; love is not envious or boastful or arrogant or rude. It does not insist on its own way; it not irritable or resentful; it does not rejoice in wrongdoing, is but rejoices in the truth. It bears all things, believes all things, hopes all things, endures all things.

Love never ends. But as for prophecies, they will come to an end; as for tongues, they will cease; as for knowledge, it will come to an end. For we know only in part, and we prophesy only in part; but when the complete comes, the partial will come to an end. When I was a child, I spoke like a child, I thought like a child, I reasoned like a child; when I become an adult, I put an end to childish ways. For now we see in a mirror, dimly, but then we will see face to face. Now I know only in part; then I will know fully, even as I have been fully known. And now faith, hope, and love abide, these three; and the greatest of these is love.

—1 Corinthians 13:1–13

A Simple Meditation. Try this meditation from the Dalai Lama. As you breathe in, say, "May I cherish myself." As you breathe out, say, "May I cherish others." Spend five minutes on this meditation at the beginning of each day. Notice that in this meditation and the one that follows, you start with loving yourself, then move to loving others.

Loving Kindness Meditation. This meditation can be used any time— as a way to start the morning, at night in the quiet of your bedroom, or while you are vacuuming, walking the dog, riding an exercise bike, or pulling weeds in your garden. Say to yourself three times:

May I be filled with loving kindness.
May I be well.
May I be peaceful and at ease.
May I be happy.

Then replace the word "I" with "you," thinking of a friend, and say it three times. You may want to repeat this round over and over, thinking of various friends. You may also want to say it three times while thinking of someone you are struggling with in some way. Finally, substitute the word "we," thinking of a group you are part of.

Journaling Suggestions. Make a list of people you think of as your friends, past and present. Put a star by those who fit this definition of a friend: someone with whom you share your soul, your innermost being, the depth of your life. Underline your all-time best friends. How did this feel?

To what extent did you come to this group looking for friends? Has it worked?

When, if ever, did you learn that you had to give your friends space to be themselves? When, if ever, did you feel that you needed more space? If you have ever had to ask for better boundaries in a relationship, how did the other person respond?

Write about a time when you were hurt deeply by a friend or hurt a friend. Did you work through the hurt?

Instead of giving advice and fixing our problems, some friends are able to listen with an open heart. If you have experienced this kind of friend, how did those moments feel? If you have tried to be that kind of friend, how did that go?

Think about a friendship you are willing to talk about with the group. In the gathering, you will be asked to briefly tell about one of your all-time best friends. This person might not necessarily be a soul mate, but does have a special place in your heart.

GATHERING

Candle Lighting

Blessed is the fire that burns deep in the soul. It is the flame of the human spirit touched into being by the mystery of life. It is the fire of reason; the fire of compassion; the fire of community; the fire of justice; the fire of faith. It is the fire of love burning deep in the human heart; the divine glow in every life.

—Eric Heller

On Our Hearts   10 minutes

Silence   3 minutes

Shared Readings

Friendship (is) the bond through which the living share deeply the mystery of existence and prepare themselves for the challenge of death. Only love and friendship make sense out of life, only friendship and love are strong enough to vanquish the black knight of death. If mysticism is to be found anywhere in the universe, it is wherever ordinary men and women touch the core of life by entering into the simple and abiding mysteries, such as falling in love, living their truth, or facing into death itself.

—Eugene Kennedy

When we honestly ask ourselves which person in our lives means the most to us, we often find that it is those who, instead of giving advice, solutions, or cures, have chosen rather to share our pain and touch our wounds with a warm and tender hand. The friend

who can be silent with us in a moment of despair or confusion, who can stay with us in an hour of grief and bereavement, who can tolerate not knowing, not curing, not healing and face with us the reality of our powerlessness, that is a friend who cares.
—Henri Nouwen

For none of us ever really walks in another's shoes or knows the innermost rooms of a person's heart. None of us truly knows the lonely places of another's journey or the causes of the lines around another's eyes. Therefore, let us be gentle with one another. Let us listen more than we speak and accept more than we judge. Let our open, outstretched hands reach and touch that we may walk along together for a little while in friendship and in trust.
—Elizabeth Tarbox

Sharing   60 minutes

Closing Activity

Tokens of Friendship

Closing Words

A friend is one to whom one may pour out all the contents of one's heart, chaff and grain together, knowing that the gentlest of hands will take and sift it, keep what is worth keeping and with a breath of kindness blow the rest away.
—Dinah Craik

Conclude the gathering by singing "Thank You for Your Loving Hands" (page xii) and making any necessary announcements.

Doubt

∾

BEFORE YOU GATHER

There lives more faith in honest doubt, believe me, than in half the creeds.
　　—Alfred Tennyson

The courage to be is rooted in the God who appears when God has disappeared in the anxiety of doubt.
　　—Paul Tillich

Whether your faith is that there is a God or that there is not a God, if you don't have any doubts, you are either kidding yourself or asleep. Doubts are the ants in the pants of faith. They keep it awake and moving.
　　—Frederick Buechner

Faith and doubt, both are needed.
　　—Lillian Smith

Believe those who are seeking the truth. Doubt those who find it.
　　—André Gide

The depth of man's questioning is more important than his answers.

—André Malraux

Underlying all life is the ground of doubt and self-questioning which sooner or later must bring us face to face with the ultimate meaning of our life.

—Thomas Merton

Consider This

Have you ever been called a Doubting Thomas? Too often that accusation is thrown at those who have questions and doubts about orthodox theologies, as if it is a character flaw or a kind of willful blindness. So it's ironic that the original Doubting Thomas was one of Jesus' disciples, and that according to the story, Jesus treated him with great respect.

The story is in the book of John. It was written some seventy years after the death of Jesus and is probably one of the legends developed in the early church rather than a historical account, but it is a great story.

On Easter evening (that is, three days after Jesus' brutal death on the cross), all of the grieving disciples, except Thomas, were gathered in a second-story room behind a locked door. To their shock, Jesus came through the door and greeted them. He soothed their disbelief by letting them see his wounded hands and side, then gave them instructions for their ministry in the world and disappeared.

When Thomas rejoined his friends, he was greeted with the most incredible story about the appearance and words of a man he knew was dead. Thomas's reaction was just about what yours or mine would be: "No way! You all are crazed by grief." When pressed to accept the evidence of his friends' experience, he refused with admirable integrity. "Not till I've seen him myself!" Thomas said, "Not till I've put my finger into the nail-holes in his hands will I believe this."

The next Sunday night, the disciples were gathered in a locked room again, and this time Thomas was with them. We have to stop and admire him for this. He could have been so threatened by the new and outlandish beliefs of his friends that he refused to have anything to do with them. Apparently, however, Thomas was willing to trust his friends and put himself in the position to share what they had learned. He was not to be disappointed, according to the story. Again, Jesus appeared and greeted them. Then he said to Thomas, very sympathetically, "Reach your finger here; see my hands. Reach your hand here and put it into my side. Live unbelieving no longer, but live believing."

The story says that Thomas, faced with evidence of Jesus' resurrection, became a believer. The integrity that caused him to resist believing on evidence of others' experience required him to believe when he had the experience himself. He was a skeptic by nature, apparently, but open to new experiences and willing to be changed by them.

Opening Ourselves to Experience. This is a kind of faithful agnosticism. The fact that this story was told in the early church and included in one of the gospels suggests that the early church was aware of doubt and sympathetic to the problems of believing what one can't see. Remember, this is a parable—a story told not because it happened, but because it has something to teach us about how to live. You don't have to believe in Jesus' resurrection to appreciate the point of the story. The story reminds us that when Thomas got his evidence, he was open-minded and flexible enough to affirm his experience and change what he believed.

Not all of us are able to be as flexible as Thomas. When confronted by new evidence, we tend to want to stick to our old opinions and beliefs, at least while we gather corroborating evidence and take some time to adjust. But if we are on a journey of integrity, adjust we must. This is the heart of Jesus' invitation to Thomas to "live unbelieving no longer, but live believing."

Maybe you once believed that homosexuality is a problem of mental health—until you met a gay man as sound in mind and spirit as yourself. Or you believed that God answers all sincere prayers, but your grandmother died in spite of yours. Or you were taught that chiropractors are quacks, but your spouse's backaches were cured that way. As you amass new experiences and begin to doubt your old beliefs, you are "living unbelieving." It is easy to just push the doubts back and forget about it, but a better way is to give yourself time to adjust, discern, test a new belief, or embrace a new truth. This takes time and energy and is rarely comfortable. It takes great integrity to stay in this gray zone until you find your new (or old, but tested) beliefs again.

The Benefit of Doubt. The Buddha insisted that an attitude of doubt is necessary, because some things do not come with proof. It is written that he said the following to one of his disciples, a man named Kalamas:

> It is proper that you have doubt, that you have perplexity, for a doubt has arisen in a matter which is doubtful. Now, look you Kalamas, do not be led by reports, or tradition, or hearsay. Be not led by the authority of religious texts, nor by mere logic or inference, nor by considering appearances, nor by the delight in speculative opinions, nor by seeming possibilities; nor by the idea: "this is our teacher." But, O Kalamas, when you know for yourself that certain things are unwholesome and wrong and bad, then give them up.
> . . . And when you know for yourself that certain things are wholesome and good, then accept them and follow them.

Let's take it as a given, then, that our lives will and should contain the experience of doubting what others believe. Here are three variations on the universal theme of doubt.

Doubt as a Theology. Gnostic is a Greek word that means "knowledge of God." Agnostic comes from *gnostic* and means "no knowledge of God." A through-and-through agnostic claims that by the nature of things, we can't completely understand God, at least not for sure. Although some people use the word "agnostic" to mean that they themselves don't know much about God, technically agnosticism is a belief about the nature of the world we live in. One way of parsing out the scale of religiously conservative to religiously liberal is on a scale of agnosticism. Generally speaking, the more conservative and fundamentalist one is, the more specific one's beliefs and the more sure one is about them. Liberals tend to be more modest about their theological claims, more aware of the limits of their knowledge, and in consequence, more accepting of differing views. Agnosticism finds it easy to be tolerant and difficult to be concrete in matters of faith.

Religious liberals are much more likely than religious conservatives to stand firm on the right and responsibility of individuals to think out religious matters for themselves and to base their beliefs on their own experience. For these people, a theology of agnosticism is required by their integrity—until and unless they have had the experiences that would lead them to faith.

Doubt as a Dodge. Most people find religious belief hard. That still, small voice is not only soft, it speaks seldom. Sorting out what we believe is work. Not everyone cares enough to do the work. Most are content to let others do the hard thinking. Folks like this might be members of orthodox churches; they don't really believe, but they don't care enough to kick up a fuss or try to find something else. Some agnostics are content to shrug and say "I don't know." But in reality, they don't care. At this time in their lives, their concerns are not theological, and they give little attention to sorting out matters of faith.

Doubt as Development. Those who study the way people grow in faith say that there is an appropriate stage when doubt reigns. As persons enter their teens, they become able to sort out what they believe from what beloved others have told them is true. They want proofs and insist on using their own minds. Too often, these youth discover that the adults around them are not charmed by theological independence. As a result, the youth often part company with church as soon as they can. Later in their life, they begin to soften their skepticism and give more credence to their emotions and intuitions, sometimes returning to a less literal, more sophisticated version of their childhood faith—just in time to be discomfited by their own teenager's budding doubts.

Doubting Thomas, you see, was quite an admirable character—firm in his convictions and able to change when confronted by new experiences. He insisted on seeing for himself, but he was willing to go where he might be changed. He let himself be curious rather than threatened by the beliefs of others. He's one of the patron saints of liberal religion.

Activities

Before the gathering, reflect on doubt by doing one or more of the following activities.

Doubts in the Psalms. Here is an adaptation of one psalm that speaks about doubt. As you read it, consider the kinds of doubts that sneak into your day. Make a list. Do you find any recurring themes in the list of your doubts?

> I am angry with myself.
> I feel weak and fearful.
> I'm beset with conflicts, inside and out—
> paralyzed, shaky, sleepless, tearful.
> How long must I endure this, God? What's the point?
> Is it a test? Do you care? Are you there?
> I can never prove you are there,
> I only know that I feel lighter for having asked.
> It comes to me, what I could do next—
> that some of my conflicts can be put aside.
> Then I can face all that I need to do.
> I'm not so confused anymore.
> —Psalm 6, adapted by Christine Robinson

To Know You. Consider the following poem. Do you find it hard to share your doubts? Why? What baffles you that you are willing to share with the group?

> To Know You
>
> Don't tell me your answers . . .
> Tell me your doubts.
> Don't drag out your expertise . . .
> Tell me what baffles you.
> Let me wander around in your realness
> Not in your carefully mended mask.
> —Alicia Hawkins

Pencils and Pens. Artists often begin a drawing with a pencil, using their eraser liberally. When they are happy with their drawing, they "ink it in," using a pen to make it permanent. You can do something similar with old and new beliefs and doubts. Begin by making a list of words that evoke old and current beliefs and doubts, both religious and other, from the Tooth Fairy to God to alternative medicine. Using a pencil, arrange them on a blank page in some artistic way, varying their size, weight, and placement to indicate their importance in your life. Keep those beliefs and doubts you have left behind in pencil, but "ink in" the beliefs you feel sure of with a colored marker.

Journaling Suggestions. Make a list of some of the things you used to believe that you now doubt (religious and nonreligious, from "Sinners go to hell" to "If he loves me, he'll go to bed at the same time I do every night"). What made the change for you?

Think about some of the things you believe and where those beliefs come from. How much weight do you give to your experience versus the experience of others?

Is there anyone in your life now who encourages you to doubt or who listens without judgment when you express your doubts?

How do you respond to that? If you are an encourager of questioning for others, how do they respond?

What are some things (religious and nonreligious) that people around you believe but you doubt? How does your doubt affect your relationships with those who believe?

How are faith, belief, certainty, and doubt related in your life? How do you feel about the idea that doubt is a good thing for faith?

If you are questioning your theology at this time in your life, what are some of the questions you are focusing on?

Think of some doubts you are struggling with now. Decide which ones you are willing to share with the group and how you will do that. Also jot down one or two in the form of questions—such as "What should I be doing with my life?"—to share with the group anonymously.

∽

GATHERING

Candle Lighting

Come we now out of the darkness of our unknowing
　　and the dusk of our dreaming;
Come we now from far places.
Come we now into the twilight of our awakening
　　and the reflection of our gathering.
Come we now all together.

We bring, unilluminated, our dark caves of doubting;
We seek, unbedazzled, the clear light of understanding.
May the sparks of our joining kindle our resolve,

brighten our spirits, reflect our love,
and unshadow our days.
Come we now; enter the dawning.
   —Annie Foerster

On Our Hearts   10 minutes

Silence   3 minutes

Shared Readings

I think everybody knows what it's like to be Thomas. . . . Thomas is
a patron saint for those of us who are trying to live a critical faith.
He is not satisfied with other people's accounts: he wants to know
by experience. He wants his religion to be his own. He wants to
touch the truth for himself, and until then, maybe even in spite
of himself, he says he will not believe. . . . Thomas's religion is a
critical *faith*.
   —Chris Walton

Cherish your doubts, for doubt is the handmaiden of truth. Doubt
is the key to the door of knowledge; it is the servant of discovery.
A belief which may not be questioned binds us to error, for there
is incompleteness and imperfection in every belief. Doubt is the
touchstone of truth; it is an acid which eats away the false. Let no
man fear for the truth, that doubt may consume it; for doubt is
a testing of belief. The truth stands boldly and unafraid; it is not
shaken by testing: for truth, if it be truth, arises from each testing
stronger, more secure.
   —Robert T. Weston

I would like to beg you, dear Sir, as well as I can, to have patience with everything unresolved in your heart and to try to love *the questions themselves* as if they were locked rooms or books written in a very foreign language. Don't search for the answers, which could not be given to you now, because you would not be able to live them. And the point is, to live everything. *Live* the questions now. Perhaps then, someday far in the future, you will gradually, without even noticing it, live your way into the answer.

—Rainer Maria Rilke

Sharing   60 minutes

Closing Activity

Sharing Unresolved Beliefs

Closing Words

Question your convictions, for beliefs too tightly held strangle
    the mind and its natural wisdom.
Suspect all certitudes, for the world whirls on—nothing abides.
Yet in our inner rooms full of doubt, inquiry and suspicion, let a
    corner be reserved for trust.
For without trust there is no space for communities to gather or
    for friendships to be forged.
Indeed, this is the small corner where we connect—and reconnect
    —with each other.

—Michael A. Schuler

Conclude the gathering by singing "Thank You for Your Loving Hands" (page xii) and making any necessary announcements.

Making Peace with Parents

∾

BEFORE YOU GATHER

Our relationship with our parents is the "original" relationship of our lives, the template for all other connections.
—Dale Atkins

In magical thinking, we wish the good and pleasurable aspects of life would last forever. Nothing on our bodies would ever sag or wrinkle; our children would always adore us; our parents would never grow old and die. Nor would we grow old and die.
—Joan Gattuso

In the beginning there was my mother. A shape. A shape and a force, standing in the light. You could see her energy; it was visible in the air. Against any background she stood out.
—Marilyn Krysl

It doesn't matter who my father was; it matters who I remember he was.
—Anne Sexton

My mother was dead for five years before I knew that I had loved her very much.
—Lillian Hellman

When the strongest words for what I have to offer come out of me sounding like words I remember from my mother's mouth, then I either have to reassess the meaning of everything I have to say now, or re-examine the worth of her old words.
—Audre Lorde

If I am self-differentiated—in other words if I have a clear sense of my own self—I will know where I end and you begin.
—Roger Bertschausen

Compassion for our parents is the true sign of maturity.
—Anaïs Nin

All your life you've envisioned your parent as strong and powerful, so as he or she gets weaker and more dependent, barriers begin to fall away.
—Hugh Delehanty and Elinor Ginzler

Consider This

One of the most important tasks of adult life is to come to terms with our parents—to appreciate what needs appreciating, understand what needs understanding, and forgive what needs forgiving. This work is sometimes called "self-differentiation." It allows us to see our background with some dispassion, to see our parents as the persons they really are and were, with their gifts and flaws and quirks and love. This in turn allows us to claim what is true to us and leave the rest behind, which strengthens our own sense of self and personal meaning.

Children depend on their parents for their very being, and in their minds, they need much more than any parent can give. As early as age two, they begin to resent their parents' power over them and attempt to assert themselves against it (a process repeated at least twice, during adolescence and young adulthood). Oh, what mixed emotions this struggle leaves us with, even when we were blessed with wise, attentive parents! If our parents were struggling with their own difficulties, we have even more mixed emotions about them. We needed them to be perfect.

The Whole Picture. We want to honor our parents, but that's hard for the little child in us to do if that child is struggling with hurts and resentments. Some people have a pervasive belief that they didn't get enough attention or care as children. They may find it helpful to ask themselves what was missing. Did their father hide behind the newspaper every night? Were they not taken to the doctor when they were ill? Did no one come to school plays or ball games? Once the list is made, it's helpful to get a more complete picture. Other family members may have additional memories or information about some of these incidents or behaviors. Conversations and gentle questions that start with the assumption that everyone was doing the best they could often bring healing information to light.

People who learn unexpected facts about their parents not only understand their childhoods better, but gain a wiser perspective on their parents. They are able to see them as ordinary people—flawed, trying, failing, and precious. In addition, many adults have healed their relationships with difficult parents through prayer or meditation. Praying for people, or simply holding their images in your mind while holding love in your heart, are exercises that have remarkable powers to change our perspective and allow us to let go of past hurts.

A New Reality. A second aspect of honoring our parents involves looking at our own needs, expectations, and behavior in light of current reality. For many of us, that reality is that our parents now need us, a need that will likely continue to increase as they age. This can be hard to accept. It confronts our inner child's desire for constant parenting from perfect parents, and also confronts our grown-up self with demands to fit more into our already demanding lives. The inner child—who still wants the total care and attention we had as infants (but with all the autonomy and choices we now enjoy as adults)—must find an inner parent who can nurture, soothe, and motivate. The present adult must care for our parents in spite of the reality that those parents can still hurt us.

Honoring our parents, then, is not just a matter of forgiving our parents. It is a matter of getting real with ourselves. It's a matter of walking a mile in our parents' shoes, both retracing their steps in the past and understanding their current path. It is a matter of taking responsibility for our feelings and letting others be who they are.

Activities

Before the gathering, reflect on your parents (or other adults who were parent figures in your life) by doing one or more of the following activities.

Draw a Genogram. A genogram is a diagram similar to a family tree, but it shows the emotional relationships in a family from one person's perspective. The starting point is marked "me." From it, lines are drawn to other family members, such as parents, siblings, spouses, and children. The emotional relationship between two persons is indicated by the type of line that connects them. The chart below indicates the meanings of the types of lines.

one solid line	_____	a normal relationship
two solid lines	══════	a close relationship
a slash in the line	____/____	separated
two slashes in the line	___//____	divorced
a dotted line	………..	indifferent/apathetic relationship
a dashed line interrupted by two slashes	- - - // - - -	an estranged relationship
a jagged line	/\/\/\/\/	a hostile relationship
a colored jagged line	/\/\/\/\/	an abusive relationship

Below is a sample genogram of a woman (marked "me") with a divorced husband. She has two siblings: a brother she is very close to and a sister from whom she is estranged. She has a hostile relationship with her father-in-law. She has two children and is closer to the elder than the younger.

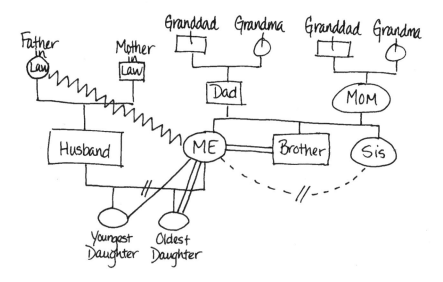

Draw your own genogram. Make up variations in the symbols and lines to suit your needs.

Explore an Early Memory. Check in with your siblings or extended family about a strong early memory. You may want to jot down your recollections before you contact them.

Get Answers. If one or both of your parents are living, call or write to ask a question that has troubled you.

Write a Letter. If you have a deceased parent or are estranged from a parent, try writing a letter to him or her (which you don't intend to send—this is for you). You might express your love, ask questions, or rant and rave. If there are unresolved issues, you may want to write the letter twice: the first time to express your feelings, and the second time to reflect on the situation more objectively.

Journaling Suggestions. What were some of the major principles your parents (or parent figures) taught you? Examples might include how one approaches the issues of honesty, life purpose, God, hard work, happiness, loving, caring for others, compassion, or safety.

What is one endearing memory you have of your parents or parent figures as you were growing up? What is one difficult memory you have?

How are you like each of your parents or other important family members in your life? How are you different?

If you have been a parent, when did you notice yourself acting like your parents did? In what ways, if any, has being a parent affected your relationship with your own parents?

Have you had to become your parents' parent in any way? If not, have you thought about the possibility? How do you feel about it?

If you have a partner, what is your relationship with your partner's parents?

If you have had stepparents, what is (or was) that relationship like?

Are your parents still serving as teachers, mentors, or role models (good or bad) for you now? In what ways?

Think about a memory of each of your parents, or other important adults in your life, as you were growing up. It may be a pleasant or difficult memory. Choose one that you are willing to share with the group.

~

GATHERING

Candle Lighting

May the Light of Truth illumine our minds,
May the Spark of Love set our hearts on fire,
May the Flame of Freedom burn brightly within us,
Now and always.
  —Richard M. Fewkes

On Our Hearts   10 minutes

Silence   3 minutes

Shared Readings

Our relationship with our parents . . . plays itself out in our romances,
in our friendships, and in the way we deal with our own children.
It's the cradle in which our concept of intimacy was born—the
need for approval, the nagging sense that we're being either smoth-
ered or rejected, the fear that we are, at some basic level, not really
loved . . . or clutched too tightly to breathe. No wonder it's so hard
to figure out how much weight to give the past when we're trying to
figure out how to deal with our parents today.
  —Dale Atkins

Getting beyond blame does not mean exonerating people from the
part they play or played in the creation of a problem. It means seeing the total picture, acquiring a balanced view—not feeling com-
pelled to either approve or disapprove of the nature of one's own
and other people's families.
  —Murray Bowen and Michael Kerr

Reconciling after an estrangement is one of the most gratifying things we can do. Reestablishing trust after it has been broken is a gutsy, difficult challenge, and those who accomplish it are rewarded with a deeper sense of compassion, restored faith in human decency, and renewed bonds of love. . . . Being able to care for aging parents without resentment is a common benefit of reconciliation.

—Laura Davis

Sharing   60 minutes

Closing Activity

The Ideal Inner Parent

Closing Words

These years can be about reconciliation, understanding, and acceptance. If this stage in all our lives is handled properly, we may experience epiphanies and sparkling moments when we see and love each other as we truly are. At last, after decades of squabbling, we may be able to get things right.

—Hugh Delehanty and Elinor Ginzler

Conclude the gathering by singing "Thank You for Your Loving Hands" (page xii) and making any necessary announcements.

Sustainable Living

∾

BEFORE YOU GATHER

What is the use of a house if you haven't got a tolerable planet to put it on?
—Henry David Thoreau

Our task must be to free ourselves from this prison by widening our circle of compassion to embrace all living creatures.
—Albert Einstein

"It's a question of discipline," the little prince told me later on. "When you've finished washing and dressing each morning, you must tend your planet."
—Antoine de Saint-Exupéry

We must describe with our lives the future we want to see for our children.
—Rich Heffern

We need to be the change we wish to see in the world.
—Mahatma Gandhi

Consider This

Perhaps you remember the story from A. A. Milne's book *Winnie-the-Pooh* in which Pooh visits Rabbit, squeezing his rotund figure through Rabbit's hole. He eats so much of Rabbit's honey that when it comes time to leave, he becomes stuck halfway out. Christopher Robin is summoned to this emergency. After pushing and pulling, he proclaims that the problem will be cured only by a week of dieting, in place. Pooh is naturally distraught by this news, and a sympathetic Christopher Robin says that he will read to his friend to pass the time. Pooh sighs, a tear rolls down his cheek, and he says, "Then would you read a Sustaining Book, such as would help and comfort a Wedged Bear in Great Tightness?"

Our Great Tightness. We who consume so large a share of the planet's resources and who add so much carbon dioxide and other greenhouse gases to the atmosphere are also in a Great Tightness. We like our lifestyle, with its inexpensive trinkets, fresh food from all over the planet, personal mobility, and toss-away conveniences. We are beginning to wake up to the fact that we are getting too fat to live on the planet, that we are not living in a sustainable way and are going to have to start doing so. It's a many-faceted problem and will likely have many solutions, some easy, some difficult, some painful, some, perhaps, unexpectedly sweet. As we contemplate the losses, sacrifices, and challenges of climate change and the dwindling of fossil fuel resources, we should also contemplate what it really means to live a sustainable lifestyle.

What Really Sustains. Sustainability and *sustenance* are big, deep words. Sustenance, when applied to food, means more than just vitamins and calories. Sustenance implies food that maintains not only our physical lives but our whole lives—food that tastes good, is good for us, was cooked and served with love, and is eaten in community. Mere calories do not sustain. Honey is not the meaning of life. What really sustains us is having a friend who will read to you while you recover from your foolishness, and who will read the kind of sustaining book that will speak to the depth of your being and remind you of what really gives you joy and meaning.

Living a sustainable lifestyle is an ethical matter of not taking more than one gives back, of living so that others in the world and future generations will have the means of living. There's satisfying, sustaining purpose in living an ethical life. Living sustainably also means living a life that is truly sustaining—that is, a life of real depth, warmth, and purpose. The two matters are related. If we've nothing truly sustaining in our lives, then why would we forgo any comfort, gratification, or whim for others or for the future? Without the sustenance that learning, beauty, love, and faith give us, the journey to ecological sustainability will seem nothing but sacrifice and "stuckness," and we'll have to be dragged to it, kicking and screaming all the way.

Steps Toward Hope. Perhaps you have already begun a sustainability "diet" in small or large ways. You may have purchased a car that gets good gas mileage, compact fluorescent lightbulbs, or energy- and water-saving appliances. Perhaps you have started hanging out a load of wash in good weather, recycling, or sharing rides to work. These efforts may seem very small, but they further a movement, create new markets, and signal to politicians that people are serious about these issues.

Perhaps just as importantly, these efforts prevent despair. Despair is always a shortsighted emotion, a faithless and hopeless and often loveless stance toward the future. A sustainable approach to climate change turns its back on despair and gets to work. The situation is not hopeless for the human race as a whole, and probably not even for civilization as we know it. We need to remember that the solution to almost every environmental crisis we've faced so far has disrupted our lives far less than was initially projected. When acid rain started killing the eastern forests thirty years ago, governments got serious about air pollution, and now the forests are beginning to thrive again. The cost was only about 10 percent of what was projected. We drive affordable cars emitting only 2 percent of the pollutants that cars from the 1970s emitted. Emissions of CFCs, chemical compounds that deplete the ozone layer, have been virtually eliminated from our technology. Our rivers no longer catch on fire. Most of us have home recycling. Slow and clumsy as our governmental processes are, we do know how to regulate industry and commerce and even lifestyles when it is clear that we need to. While we wait for political solutions to problems of sustainable lifestyle (and do our part to bring them about), we can celebrate the sustaining satisfaction of being mindful and thrifty about how we use energy and resources.

Sustaining Values. The Wedged Bear will get over his despair, and he will probably scrabble a bit. Who could resist the temptation to make the hole bigger rather than the tummy smaller? But what will make the time of the diet bearable in the end is sustaining values, of which honey is not one. The time will be made bearable by good friends and good books, the things that really nourish Pooh's life.

It will be the same for us. As we pare down to a sustainable lifestyle, what will sustain us is education, spiritual growth, love, and community. These are all are very ecological enterprises—low in resource use, virtually nonpolluting, and most importantly, sustaining us in a way that baubles and bangles never will. If it becomes impossibly expensive to drive across town to shop, we will fall back on the truly sustaining pastimes of conversation, learning, meditation, and caring for and about those who are close by. If we can no longer hop a plane to visit friends and relations whenever we wish, we will relearn the art of letter writing, though it will probably be through email. If we can no longer eat South American plums in the dead of winter, we will rediscover local food and the fresh joys of conversation.

The unsustainable ways we have been living for the past several generations are catching up with us very quickly now, and the crisis of change has already begun. There are already small island nations in the South Pacific that are nearly under water, people suffering from cancer, dry wells, new and terrible diseases taking advantage of weakened populations, and livelihoods challenged by high gas prices. The solutions to the problems we have created will no doubt require sacrifice, ingenuity, and adaptation to change. What will carry us through the times of difficulty and paring down will be the sustaining values of learning, faith, and community.

Activities

Before the gathering, reflect on sustainable living by doing one or more of the following activities.

Save Water and Energy. Read the following list of ways to conserve water. Put a check by the ones you already do. Star the ones you will try this week. Put a question mark by the ones you want to think about incorporating into your life. Add any other ideas you come up with.

- Reduce your shower time to five minutes.
- Install a low-flow showerhead.
- Air-dry your dishes instead of heat-drying them.
- Get an aerator for your kitchen faucet.
- Consider washing and rinsing all clothes in cold water.
- Reduce the number of loads of wash you do per week. (Can you wear anything an extra time?)
- Set your water heater thermostat to 120 degrees Fahrenheit.
- Catch rainwater in barrels as it flows off the house.
- Plant more indigenous plants and less grass around your home.
- Turn off the faucet when you brush your teeth.
- Repair leaking faucets and toilets.
- Use a bucket instead of a running hose to wash the car.

Pare Down. Walk around your home, making note of how many electrical appliances and devices you have. How many of these are really necessary to a satisfying life? Explore ways to pare down by taking unneeded items to recycling centers, garage sales, or resale shops. Of the items you need, how many stay on all the time? They are still using electricity even when they are "on standby." Develop the habit of unplugging these items when not in use.

Join with Others. Being "green" is very prominent these days. Look for groups with sustainable living as a goal, and consider joining one. You'll become more aware of ways to save the planet, get to know like-minded people, and support one another's efforts. Try finding groups at churches, your children's schools, or in your neighborhood. Can't find a group? Start one!

Journaling Suggestions. What lifestyle changes or choices have you made for the good of the planet? Are there lifestyle changes you think you should make, but have not? What keeps you from making them? What would help you make them?

What worries you most about the future of the earth and its ecology?

What sustains you in life that is not part of the material world? What do you think will sustain you if our society goes through a period of environmental belt-tightening?

A sustainable life is one of not taking more than we give back. What are some ways you can give back?

How we solve the problems created by global warming will depend on our answers to fundamentally spiritual questions. What is the nature of a good life? What is the purpose of this life we have been given? Who are my brothers/sisters/neighbors, and what is my responsibility to them? Reflect on these questions in your journal.

Think about your "sustainability diet." What changes will you consider making for a more sustainable lifestyle? What will sustain you in the process? Think about what you are willing to share with the group.

∽

GATHERING

Candle Lighting

We light this candle
To illuminate the world we seek.
In the search for truth, may we be just;
In the search for justice, may we be loving;
And, in loving, may we find peace.
　　—Elizabeth McMaster

On Our Hearts　　10 minutes

Silence　　3 minutes

Shared Readings

When the animals come to us,
asking for our help,
will we know what they are saying?
When the plants speak to us,
in their delicate, beautiful language,
will we be able to answer them?
When the planet herself

sings to us in our dreams,
will we be able to wake ourselves,
and act?
   —Gary Lawless

In today's highly interdependent world, individuals and nations can no longer resolve many of their problems by themselves. We need one another. We must, therefore develop a sense of universal responsibility. . . . It is our collective and individual responsibility to protect and nurture the global family, to support its weaker members and to preserve and tend to the environment in which we all live.
   —The Dalai Lama

What we call little things are merely the causes of great things; they are the beginning, the embryo, and it is the point of departure which, generally speaking, decides the whole future of an existence. One single black speck may be the beginning of a gangrene, of a storm, of a revolution.
   —Henri Frédéric Amiel

As individuals living on the planet at this moment in time, we face a challenge no generation has ever had to face. We need to dramatically change the manner in which we use the Earth's natural resources. . . . If the bad news is that individual Americans are a major part of the problem, the good news is that we can also be a major part of the solution.
   —David Gershon

Sharing   60 minutes

Closing Activity
Sharing Insights

Closing Words

I pledge allegiance to the earth and all life:
the fields and streams, the mountains and seas,
the forests and deserts, the air and soil,
all species and reserves, habitats and environments;
one world, one creation, one home, indivisible for all,
affected by pollution anywhere, depleted by any waste,
endangered by greedy consumption, degradation by faithlessness;
preserved by recycling, conservation, and reverence,
the great gift renewed for all generations to come,
protected, preserved by reducing, reusing, recycling.
With conservation and reverence,
the great gift renewed for all generations to come.
    —Vern Barnet

Conclude the gathering by singing "Thank You for Your Loving Hands"
(page xii) and making any necessary announcements.

Endings

∾

BEFORE YOU GATHER

Great is the art of beginning, but greater the art is of ending.
—Henry Wadsworth Longfellow

Behind a Good-bye there lurks much of the salutation of another beginning.
—Walt Whitman

Our lives are full of transitions. We sometimes find ourselves in a time of simultaneous endings and beginnings. We benefit by taking the opportunity to mark these important turning points with awareness, reflection and appreciation.
—Julie Kain

What is born will die,
What has been gathered will be dispersed.
—Sogyal Rinpoche

All endings, in a way, remind us of the finality of our own.
—Steven Winn

So comes snow after fire, and even dragons have their ending.
—J.R.R. Tolkien

It is when one first sees the horizon as an end that one first begins to see.
—Archibald MacLeish

Our time together will be a chapter in the stories of our lives.
—Danita Nolan

Consider This

Our lives contain at least as many goodbyes as hellos, and not just to people. We say goodbye to our college years, to projects, to events. We say goodbye to tasks, jobs, and to people as they change. The parents of a five-year-old will have their daughter living in their house for a long time to come, but as they write the last words in her baby book, they must say goodbye not only to her as a baby, but to themselves as the parents of a baby. When you leave a job, you say goodbye not only to coworkers and clients, but to a part of your life, and perhaps even to the social role of being an employed person. Sometimes we say goodbye with glee, sometimes with true sadness; but many goodbyes are emotionally significant transitions in our lives.

The Need to Say Goodbye. The French and German words *au revoir* and *auf Wiedersehen* are translated as "goodbye," but they really mean "until we see each other again." While it is true that our goodbyes are often just temporary, there are also real endings in our lives—moments when, even if we do see each other again, we will meet in different roles and after things have profoundly changed.

It's important to attend to the endings in our lives. The "disappear into the sunset without saying goodbye" habit may seem to prevent pain, but actually, all it does is drive pain underground where it can fester like an old infection. The skin may have healed over, but the abscess underneath is causing all kinds of mischief in the body. When we don't say our goodbyes, even though they are painful—indeed, especially when they are painful—we drive our sadness underground, where it can pool into illness, depression, or an unwillingness to start new relationships.

A good goodbye is not only a sad acknowledgement of change, but also an opportunity for gratitude and for finishing any unfinished business of the relationship. It is when we say goodbye that we realize what we valued this person for and what gifts he or she gave us. If we share that, the other person is likely to share in turn, so that we hear what gifts we gave.

When a relationship really is over, or over in this particular form, it is more appropriate to acknowledge and bless that event than to gloss it over. It is better for our mental health to deal with reality. When we are conscientious about this, we find ourselves with more good memories and less grief-soaked baggage to carry through our lives. If we are well practiced in saying goodbye, we will find all of our goodbyes a little easier, including the final goodbyes we say before we die.

An artful ending to a relationship, like the resolving chords of a symphony, often defines what has gone before. Endings are a good chance to shape the meaning of our lives. What makes for an artful ending? Ideally, it includes four components: disengagement, memory, resolution, and blessing.

Disengagement. The first step of an artful goodbye is disengagement. At some point we must acknowledge to ourselves and to the other that we may not meet again, or that if we do, it will be in changed circumstances. To gloss over this step will make the rest of the relationship feel lame. To risk taking this step will charge what comes next with significance and end the relationship on a glowing note of reality.

In "Stars, Songs, Faces," Carl Sandburg wrote:

Gather the stars if you wish it so.
Gather the songs and keep them.
Gather the faces of women.
Gather for keeping years and years.

And then . . .
Loosen your hands, let go and say good-by.
Let the stars and songs go.
Let the faces and years go.
Loosen your hands and say good-by.

What a beautiful image this is! And how often we find ourselves clenching our fists and our hearts to avoid doing what life calls us to do, which is to disengage from the past and move into the future. Loosen your hands, let go, and say goodbye.

Memory. The art of ending also includes memory—and often, sharing our memories. A good ending is one in which the relationship or experience has been remembered. That is one of the main focuses of a memorial service. There is great healing in simply remembering and telling the story of the deceased.

Resolution. Sometimes memories bring tension, and a good ending will help to resolve that tension. We might clear up what really happened, forgive a hurt, acknowledge imperfections, agree to disagree, or come to realize that we all communicated poorly and congratulate ourselves for going on with the relationship anyway. The art of ending includes attempting to come to a comfortable resting place with the relationship or situation as it really was.

Blessing. The word *goodbye* is descended from "God be with you," as is the Spanish adios. In these languages, every goodbye, even the most routine, is a blessing given to a person whom we care about.

In an artful ending, we will find a way to make our words a blessing. Those who are not comfortable with "Godspeed" or "God be with you" will perhaps adopt a significant hug, a sincere "I wish you well," or perhaps the Buddhist bow with folded hands.

With so many goodbyes in our lives, it is worth thinking through how we will make the endings that will allow us to make beginnings. For although we remain a part of all that we have met, and although nothing, not even what we have forgotten, vanishes from our inner selves, life goes on. If we are to go with it, we must learn to say goodbye.

Activities

Before the gathering, reflect on endings by doing one or more of the following activities.

Write a Letter. If there's been a particularly poor parting in your past, think about what could have made it more artful. Write a letter that begins, "If I had known that would be our last meeting . . ." or "I have learned something about saying goodbye, and if I were to do our last meeting over again . . ." You might never actually send this letter, but write it as honestly as you can.

The Garden of the Group. Think about the unique and wonderful mixture of people in your group as a garden of flowers (or vegetables). Write a poem about this garden of people you have been with for all these months. Say something about what each person has brought to the group and to you. For instance, you might write something like this:

> Our garden of blooms and buds:
> Sarah, always full of light and promise, is the daisy.
> Grace, a late blooming black-eyed susan, watches and listens to us all before she speaks her deep wisdom.
> Abby, lyrical beauty of a complex delphinium.
> John, the ground cover, who ties our stories and issues together.

If you do this exercise, you might want to make a copy of your poem for everyone in the group. As variations, artists might draw a sketch or create a collage of the "Garden of the Group."

Journaling Suggestions. Return to the Sandburg poem (page 116) and write about it. What persons, memories, or parts of yourself "gather" to be said goodbye to? Do those goodbyes include the four components described in the essay? Are there goodbyes coming up in your life that you'd like to plan for?

Write out some of your goodbye history. Write about childhood leave-takings, some of the hardest goodbyes of your life, and at least one in which you were the person who decided to say goodbye.

Consider how your body reacts to goodbyes. Some of us clench our hands when we don't want to let go. What does your body do?

Do you have a particular gesture, blessing, or turn of phrase that you like to use when saying goodbye? If so, why is it meaningful for you? If not, does anyone you know have such a ritual? If you were going to adopt one, what would it be and why?

Think about a good goodbye you have experienced in your lifetime. Consider what you are willing to share with the group about this goodbye. Also be prepared to share something you remember or appreciate about each person in the group.

∾

GATHERING

Candle Lighting

O light of life,
Be kindled again in our hearts
As we meet together
To celebrate the joy of human community
Seeking a wholeness that extends beyond us.
    —Samuel A. Trumbore

On Our Hearts   10 minutes

Silence   3 minutes

Shared Readings

The good good-bye includes: Acknowledging feelings, sharing memories, offering praise, making a promise, and giving a final blessing.
    —Danita Nolan

I wanted a perfect ending. Now I've learned, the hard way, that some poems don't rhyme, and some stories don't have a clear beginning, middle, and end. Life is about not knowing, having to change, taking the moment and making the best of it.
    —Gilda Radner

Considering that we have to deal with endings all our lives, most of us handle them very badly. This is in part because we misunderstand them and take them either too seriously or not seriously enough. We take them too seriously by confusing them with finality —that's it, all over, never more, finished! We see them as something without sequel, forgetting that in fact they are the first phase of the transition process and a precondition of self-renewal. At the same time we fail to take them seriously enough. Just because they scare us, we try to avoid them.
    —William Bridges

May this ending be our beginning.
Let us begin—again and again—
to wonder and to cherish and to act,
so that at day's end we will be content
knowing that we have given our all to life.
    —Marianne Hachten Cotter

Sharing   60 minutes

Closing Activity

Memorial Service for the Group

Closing Words

May the road rise up to meet you.
May the wind be always at your back.
May the sun shine warm upon your face;
The rains fall soft upon your fields and until we meet again,
May God hold you in the palm of His hand.
    —Gaelic blessing

Conclude the gathering by singing "Thank You for Your Loving Hands"
(page xii).

Advice for Leaders

Your basic job as leader is to take care of logistics, to prepare for special events in specific gatherings, and to keep the process feeling safe and fair to everyone in the group. You don't have to be a therapist, the authority on the topics discussed, or even the only person thinking about the health of the group. During that first session, your group will make a covenant and that will be the document to return to if things don't seem to be going right. You may have to remind your group that they all took responsibility to abide by and help others abide by the covenant. As group leader, you will help your group try this process, which will be new to most of them. Most of us are not very good about trying new things. We complain, joke, gibe, and resist. You can anticipate this and let it be okay, up to a point. You should be a cheerleader for the process until such time as the resistance gets so great that the group decides as a whole to make a change.

Preparation for Gatherings

Before each gathering, do the reading and activities listed under "Before You Gather." Also look over the leader's notes for the gathering (starting on page 129). Sometimes you will have some preparation to do, such as making copies of a picture or bringing special items to the gathering. Try to get all preparation done ahead of time, so that when people begin to arrive for the gathering you can be fully present. Some gatherings will have additional resources at our companion website, www.HeartToHeartBook.com.

Your Participation in the Group

As a leader, you are both a facilitator and a participant. Your participation is important, because you can guide by your example. Often you will go first with an exercise or sharing to show how it is done and to model sharing with depth. Go as deep as you are willing. However, some of your attention must also be focused on observing and facilitating the group process. If the topic of the gathering is so sensitive for you that you don't think you can both participate and facilitate, plan to either lighten up your sharing or ask someone else to facilitate that gathering.

Problem Members

If one member's behavior has been hurtful or difficult, you might feel the need to speak to that person between sessions. You might say something like, "John, I wonder if you realized that you talked at such length last time that others had to cut their sharing short. Is there something I can do to help you keep track of the time?" or, "Mary, remember that we have decided not to give advice to each other. Our good listening is the best gift we can give, even when someone is having as hard a time as Sue was." There may be times when one group member will come to you with a complaint about another. It's best to encourage the complainer to be direct with the person whose behavior is bothersome.

If all else fails, sometimes people have to be helped to quit the group. Meeting privately with the individual, you might say something like, "It seems that you just don't care for this process. Perhaps this is just not the right kind of group for you. If you come again, you have to live by the rules." Or you may need to be more explicit: "I'm sorry, but I must ask you to drop out of the group." It is very helpful to have another person to consult with, such as the spiritual leader of your congregation, when you get into these difficult places. Be assured that these kinds of problems don't happen very often.

Format for Gatherings

Each gathering has the same basic format, made up of the following elements. Any variations to this format are detailed in the leader's notes (starting on page 129). The notes also give approximate times for several parts of the gathering. You are encouraged to adjust the times to fit the needs of your group. While keeping time is primarily your responsibility, any member in the group may request that the group notice the time.

Candle Lighting. Ask a volunteer to do the short reading, then light the candle.

On Our Hearts. This is a time for sharing major highs and lows, not a check-in during which everyone recounts events of the week. Ask participants if anyone has a special joy or sorrow in their heart right now that they want the group to know about. Also mention any absent members.

Silence. Each gathering includes three minutes of silence. We recommend that you time it. You can set the tone for the quiet time by reading one of these quotations:

> Silence is not native to my world. Silence, more than likely, is a stranger to your world too. If you and I are ever going to have silence in our noisy hearts, we are going to have to grow it.
> —Wayne Oates

> In quietness and in trust shall be your strength.
> —Isaiah 30:15

> Speak only when we could improve on silence.
> —Sam Keen

> Silence is the language of God; it is also the language of the heart.
> —Dag Hammarskjöld

You may want to invite members to notice their breathing, feeling the breath in their nostrils or throat. You can suggest that participants try a mantra—perhaps silently repeating "be still" with each breath, or "love in" on the in-breath and "love out" on the out-breath. Or you may suggest this as a time to hold each member of the group in your hearts, remembering the remarks shared during "On Our Hearts."

The time of silence is often a completely novel concept to group members. There's bound to be some restiveness at the idea. Let the group know that you're experimenting with this too, and that you're timing it with your watch because if you didn't, you'd stop too soon. Ask the group to give it a try for three gatherings. If more than one person is still resisting after the third gathering, you can talk this over with the group. Perhaps your group just doesn't like the silence. It's also possible that when the ones who don't like it hear from the ones who do, they will be better able to tolerate this practice.

Shared Readings. You may want to go around the circle, with each person doing a reading. Or you may recruit volunteers for the readings before the gathering starts.

Sharing. Sharing is done in three rounds. Prompts for each round are in the leader's notes (starting on page 129).

In the first round, you will ask participants to share something they have learned about the topic while doing the preparation. This is a brief round of one- or two-sentence responses (about two minutes each). There may be a specific question to ask or activity to follow in the leader's notes. Go first to model for the group, then continue around the circle. This round is intended to start the process of sharing without requiring group members to go too deep. End with a moment of silence before moving on to the next round.

The second round is an opportunity for participants to share something they felt about this topic while doing the preparation— a way they grew, something that touched them, or a story they want to share. Each person has about four minutes. Go first to model for the group, then ask participants to share in any order. End with a moment of silence.

If there is time for a third round, you can be much more informal. As leader, you can start by saying how much time there is left and remind the group of the purpose of this last round ("We have about ten minutes and a chance for anyone to comment on what they've heard or any other thoughts they have on the subject. I'll start by saying that I was struck that two others had the same reaction I had . . ."). Not everyone will speak during the third round, but you'll need to notice if someone is monopolizing and help them to wind down ("We only have two more minutes, Jan, and I want to make sure no one else wants to speak . . .").

During each round, one person speaks at a time. The one who is sharing has the job of speaking deeply from the heart about the topic at hand. Listeners have the task of keeping an appreciative silence and an open heart to what is shared. If someone does not want to speak, he or she may pass.

The three-round method of sharing will be new to most group members. They will need a thorough explanation and gentle reminders as they try it for the first time. Some people will warm up to this routine only slowly, and some will dislike it at first. Encourage them to give it three tries before they give up or ask for modifications. If after three gatherings your group is still rebellious, you can drop the first sharing round and give more time to the third. In that case, you will have to take care that everyone who wants to speak during the third round has an opportunity to do so.

Part of your job as leader is to make sure that all group members get their share of talking time. You can go a long way toward accomplishing this simply by telling people how much time they have to speak and modeling time limits in your own sharing. However, you'll also want to pay attention to the clock and have a few good lines in your repertoire to help people wind up if they're taking more than their fair share of time. You might try "We want to have time for everyone, Joe, so can you wrap it up?" or "That's so interesting, Mary, but we're going to have to move along." Or you might catch the person's eye and point to your watch with a smile. Make these moves with a light touch, which is always easier if you do it before you have become irritated or the group has become restive. Only in the rarest of circumstances should you let anyone take double the allotted time. If a group member is taking too much time week after week, speak to that person about it outside of the gathering.

The emphasis in these gatherings is on telling one's own story rather than using one's time to "fix" someone else. This means no cross talk, limited questions, and equal time. Other parts of the process may be adjusted, but the ability to tell one's story and be listened to with an open heart by others is crucial; it creates the safety that is the core of the process. If someone forgets the no-cross-talk agreement, refer the group to the covenant agreed on in the first gathering. If the cross talk continues, you may want to privately remind the person of the power of telling one's story without judgment or advice from others.

During the third round, be very careful that the group does not bear down on any one member, which can feel very intimidating. If more than three comments are directed at any one person, change the focus by redirecting the conversation ("Well, we've given Les a lot to think about here. Did anyone have another thought to share before we close?"). Remind the group to speak of their own experiences rather than focusing on someone else's story.

Some groups never get to a third round of sharing. Other groups rush through the first two rounds because they really like the third round. This is fine if everyone has had the opportunity to share in depth and the group sticks to the basic rules: good listening, limited questioning, no monopolizing, and no interrupting.

If the third round seems flat or stymied, you may want to ask a question to stimulate sharing. This could be one of the following questions, or something similar: What did you discover about yourselves this evening? How are you feeling as we close this gathering? What has been most meaningful in this gathering? Then say, "Take a minute to think about this, then share with us as you are ready."

All these instructions may seem intimidating. Most groups, once they have experienced this format of sharing, come to like it and will help the leader stay focused. Your job will get easier as time goes on.

Closing Activity. This element varies from gathering to gathering. It often incorporates a simple ritual to help participants process what they have learned and shared during the gathering.

Closing Words. Unless otherwise indicated in the leader's notes, recruit someone before the gathering to read the closing words aloud.

Song. After the closing words are read, lead the group in singing "Thank You for Your Loving Hands" (see page xii). If the song is a new one to the group, you might want to practice singing it at the start of each gathering until it becomes familiar.

Announcements. At the end of each gathering, make any necessary announcements. Read the leader's notes to find out about any special items that you want participants to bring to the next gathering. Also think about seasonal considerations. At the mid-November gathering, for instance, you may want to ask whether the group would prefer a holiday social gathering, a regular gathering, or no gathering toward the end of December.

The Rewards

One of the joys of being a leader is watching the group unfold as members go deeper and grow closer. The safe environment of the group process invites and nurtures spiritual exploration and trusting bonds of friendship.

Leader's Notes for Each Gathering

These notes explain how to prepare for each gathering, describe how to facilitate the Sharing and Closing Activity segments, and provide other special instructions as needed.

LISTENING

Before the Gathering

Practice the song "Thank You for Your Loving Hands" if necessary (page xii). Read the description of the first round of sharing (see Sharing below) and think about your response so that you will be prepared to go first. Prepare a list of members' names, phone numbers, and email addresses. Place one copy of the list in the room where you will meet, along with name tags and pens.

At the Gathering

As people come in, ask them to check the list and make sure that their names, phone numbers, and email addresses are correct. Invite them to put on name tags.

Welcome and Explanations. When everyone has settled in, tell group members how glad you are that they are in the group and how much you're looking forward to getting to know them. Tell them that each gathering will last about an hour and a half to two hours. See if any group members have a need to be very strict about time (for public transportation or child care, for instance). Point out where the bathroom is. Ask members whether they are comfortable sharing their contact information with one another, and tell them that if they are, copies of the list will be provided next time.

Explain that each gathering will follow the same routine. The gathering opens with a candle lighting and On Our Hearts, which is a time for briefly sharing major highs and lows (for more on this, see page ix in the Introduction). Next comes silence and shared readings. The core of the gathering is the sharing. Describe the three rounds of sharing (see pages x–xi). Explain that there is no cross talk in the first and second rounds, but that participants are to listen deeply, from the heart. The sharing is followed by a closing activity, which is a brief ritual or exercise related to the topic. The gathering concludes with announcements, closing words, and a song. Usually announcements will be quite brief. For this gathering, they will be longer, since the group is just starting out.

Brief Introductions. Going around the circle, have members each say their name and tell one thing that drew them to this group.

Covenant and Ground Rules. Go around the circle again and let each person read a line of the covenant. Ask the group after each line: "Any comments or problems? Can we all agree to this?" Adjust the covenant to fit your needs as you go along.

Sharing. In the first round, go around the circle and ask members to share a sentence of explanation about each of their five stepping stones (15 minutes). Go first to model the sharing. For example, "This rock symbolizes the time I had cancer." In the second round, give group members the opportunity to share more deeply about one or more of their stepping stones (35 minutes). Go first to model the sharing. They can speak in any order. As time allows for the third round, those who wish to may share additional thoughts or reflect on what others have shared (10 minutes). Because this first gathering has lots of additional elements, you may not have time for the third round.

Closing Activity. Invite the group to hold hands around the circle and each share an insight they have had at this gathering or say one or two words about how they are feeling. Be prepared to go first, and proceed around the circle.

After the Gathering

If the group has agreed to share the list of contact information, prepare copies and plan to bring them to the next gathering.

GRATITUDE

Before the Gathering

Read over the instructions for the Closing Activity below. You may want to craft your sentence in advance and write yourself a little cheat sheet with the opening sentence, your sentence, and the closing sentence.

At the Gathering

Sharing. For the first round, ask the group members to find or recall the list they each made (before the gathering) of what they are grateful for. Go around the circle three or four times, giving people a chance to share some of the things on their list (15 minutes). For the second round, invite members, in any order, to share more deeply about the things for which they are grateful or their reaction to the essay, readings, or activities (35 minutes). As time allows in the third round, those who wish to may share additional thoughts or reflect on what others have shared (10 minutes).

Closing Activity. The group will create a poem together. Ask each member to create one sentence by thinking of something he or she is are grateful for, with detail—not just, "I'm grateful for my family" but, "I'm grateful to have a family that talks, laughs, and forgives." Give them time to come up with their idea. Tell them that you will begin with "We are grateful . . ." and they each complete their respective sentences by saying, " . . . for (whatever)." Go around the circle, letting each person contribute a sentence. End with your sentence, and then add the words ". . . and for all the gifts life brings." If the first time around was choppy and you have time, you might want to repeat your poem. End with the closing reading and song.

BALANCE

Before the Gathering

Read the description of the Sharing and Closing Activity segments (below) to familiarize yourself with them. Think about your response to the question in the first round of sharing so that you will be prepared to go first.

At the Gathering

Sharing. For the first round, invite group members, one at a time, to stand as they are able, stretch their arms straight out to the sides, and then raise one arm and lower the other to represent their current state of balance (with arms horizontal meaning perfectly balanced). Ask members to comment on their immediate sense of balance and a couple of areas of their lives that seem out of balance, if any. Go first to model the sharing, then go around the circle (15 minutes). In the second round, speaking in any order, members can share more deeply about the overall sense of balance in their lives or their experience with one of the activities from their preparation (35 minutes). As time allows in the third round, those who wish to may share additional thoughts or reflect on what others have shared (10 minutes).

Closing Activity. Have the group members stand far enough apart that they can all stretch out their arms to indicate their state of balance, as they did in the exercise from the first round of sharing. Ask the group members to focus inward, closing their eyes if they can do so comfortably, and think about the insights of the gathering as they experiment with a new place of balance. Tell them, "If you are feeling weighted down on one side, try lifting that up. How does that feel? What would have to change in your life to come to a new sense of balance?"

After a minute or two, draw participants back into the circle. Ask each person to share a phrase about how to come into better balance (for instance, watch less TV, get up earlier to meditate, be present to my children more). Give the group a minute to think. Be prepared to go first, and proceed around the circle.

FORGIVENESS

Before the Gathering

Bring matches and a votive candle or tea light for each member of your group (and yourself) for the closing ritual. As you set them out in your gathering space, take the time to trim or pry up the wicks so they will be easy to light.

Read the description of the first round of sharing (see below) and think about your response so that you will be prepared to go first.

Read the description of the Closing Activity segment (below). Think about a situation in your life in which you experienced willingness, but not quite readiness, to forgive. Think of a way to share this in a sentence that feels appropriate to you, such as "I am thinking about forgiving someone in my family for giving me such a hard time when my mother was dying" or "I want to forgive my father, may he rest in peace, for being such a distant dad." Be prepared to be the first one to speak to model for the group.

At the Gathering

Sharing. For the first round, invite group members to share briefly about a situation in their life in which they are struggling with whether to forgive someone. Remind the group that it is not necessary to reveal names or specific details. Go first to model for the group, and then go around the circle (15 minutes). In the second round, invite group members, in any order, to share more deeply about the situation they face, their feelings about forgiveness, or their experience with one of the activities from their preparation (35 minutes). As time allows in the third round, those who wish to share additional thoughts may reflect on what others have shared (10 minutes).

Announcements. Tell the group that you'll be departing in silence after the closing words, so this time the announcements will come before the Closing Activity ritual. Make sure that you address any logistical concerns that need to be dealt with in this part of the gathering.

Closing Activity. Ask group members to take a moment of silence, during which they think about a person they are struggling to forgive. This person may or may not be part of the situation they shared about. Acknowledge that they may be willing to forgive but feel unable to do it, or it may be a situation in which they are not yet willing to forgive.

After the silence, ask group members to come up one at a time and light a candle of forgiveness. They can choose to say nothing when they light their candle, or they can say just a few words or one sentence (no stories), such as "I forgive someone for . . ." Tell them that if they are not willing to forgive, they are invited to light a candle of hope that they will someday be willing. Remind them that they don't need to mention specific names or circumstances. Go first to model and continue around the circle.

Some people may have difficulty with this. They might balk at the instructions, giggle, or become choked up. Your role as leader is to model a nonanxious presence at whatever happens. If someone does not seem ready to light a candle, that's all right. Just ask the person if it is all right if you go on.

Closing Words. When all the candles have been lit, introduce the closing words by asking each person to read one line of the litany, with all joining in the response. Allow a brief moment of silence to let the words sink in, then say firmly "Amen" or "So be it" or whatever feels comfortable to you.

There is no song at the end of this gathering. Stand up to indicate that this is the end, and hug, hold hands, or make eye contact with all the participants as they gather their things to depart.

After the Gathering

This can be a very intense gathering. If it seems that someone in your group has had great difficulty, you might want to be in touch with him or her a few days later. One way you might help is to ask, "Have you ever thought about talking to the minister (or a therapist, counselor, or spiritual director) about this?"

GOD

Before the Gathering

Read the description of the first round of sharing (see below) and think about your response so that you will be prepared to go first.

At the Gathering

Sharing. For the first round, go around the circle and invite members to each share briefly the definition of God that most speaks to them (15 minutes). In the second round of sharing, invite members, in any order, to share more deeply on their definition of God or on their experience with one of the activities from their preparation (35 minutes). As time allows, those who wish to may share additional thoughts or reflect on what others have shared (10 minutes).

Closing Activity. Invite group members to hold hands around the circle and each say one or two words about how they are feeling or share an insight they have had at this gathering. Be prepared to go first, and proceed around the circle.

LOSS AND GRIEF

Before the Gathering

Read the description of the first round of sharing (see below) and plan how to carry out the exercise. If you have a place where your group can line up behind a starting line and walk ten to fifteen steps from there, plan to use that. If you don't have room for this, bring game markers or other tokens (such as dice, coins, or pieces of fruit) and let members move the markers on a table.

Read the description of the second round of sharing and think about your response so that you will be prepared to go first.

At the Gathering

Shared Readings. Without breaking the quiet mood, let people read the shared readings, one by one. End this by reading, yourself, the prayer found below. This prayer is an expression of hopes— whether you think that God has anything to do with this or not is irrelevant. Let this express your own hopes for the healing of the people in your group and for your own healing.

I pray for all of us who mourn.
May we face each day with courage, strength, and hope.
May nothing destroy what we have been given.
May nothing erase our memories of joy.
May all the good of the past overpower the fear of the future.
May our current laments of grief eventually change into prayers of thanksgiving.
I pray for all of us who mourn.
        —Anonymous

Sharing. For the first round (15 minutes), ask everyone to stand in a line at one end of the room (or gather around a table if you don't have enough space). Ask people to take a step forward (or move their marker on the table) each time you say something that describes them. Then read the following, adapted from *The Lessons of Loss* by Carol Galginaitis, pausing after each line:

Take a step forward (or move your marker forward) if you . . .

- have lost a loved one to illness or accident
- have moved in the last five years
- have relatives in more than three different states
- did not grow up speaking English as a first language
- have held more than four jobs
- have "put down" a pet
- have lost a favorite keepsake
- observe rituals and hold ceremonies that friends don't recognize or understand
- have totaled a car
- weren't chosen for the sports team or cast for the annual musical
- have ended an important friendship over a difference in political, personal, or religious beliefs

- have moved away from your family of origin
- are unable to do some things that were quite easy in the past (read small print, climb ladders, etc.)
- have been deeply disappointed by a close friend or relative
- have radically changed religious, moral, or political beliefs
- have immigrated to a different country
- have said goodbye to a close friend when he or she moved away
- have felt like an outsider

After you have read through the list, ask group members to notice how the string of people or markers has changed since the beginning of the exercise. Is anyone still at the starting line? Have some moved forward on most, if not all, of the statements? Think about what this tells us about the presence of loss in our lives.

For the second round of sharing, gather back in the circle and let group members share one of the losses they remembered in their preparation. Be prepared to go first to model this sharing (35 minutes). As time allows in the third round, let those who wish, speaking in any order, share more deeply of their feelings about grief and loss or share their experience with one of the activities from their preparation (10 minutes).

Closing Activity. Gather in a closer circle than you've been in, and invite group members to name a loss they are grieving or offer a few words.

Closing Words. Read the closing litany, with the whole group giving the response. Then read the following yourself:

> We bereaved are not alone. We belong to the largest company in all the world—the company of those who have known suffering. When it seems that our sorrow is too great to be borne, let us think of the great family of the heavy-hearted into which our grief has given us entrance,

and inevitably, we will feel about us their arms, their sympathy, their understanding.

—Helen Keller

Announcements. Remind the group that they are to bring a big handful of change to the next gathering.

MONEY

Before the Gathering

Remember to bring a handful of coins to this gathering. Read the descriptions of the Sharing and Closing Activity segments (below) to familiarize yourself with them.

At the Gathering

Sharing. For the first round of sharing (20 minutes), conduct the following exercise.

Ask group members to take out their handfuls of change. If someone has forgotten theirs, the group might share, or the activity can be done with any small articles at hand, such as paper clips, matches, or even torn bits of paper. Ask group members to put the coins in a pile in front of themselves. Tell them you will ask a series of questions about money and feelings, each followed by three words. If the first word describes their feelings, they should move some or all of their coins into a pile on the left. If the second word describes their feelings, they should put coins in the middle, and for the third word, coins go on the right. They can put their coins in one, two, or three piles to show the extent to which each word represents their feelings. You may want to demonstrate with a sample question.

When everyone understands what to do, read the following questions. Pause after each to give group members time to move their coins, but keep the exercise moving quickly.

1. When you were growing up, how do you think your parent(s) felt about money?

    Anxious   Calm   Oblivious

2. When you were young, how did you feel about money?

    Anxious   Calm   Oblivious

3. How do these words describe your feelings about money in the present?

    Anxious   Calm   Oblivious

4. What about these words? How do they describe your feelings about money right now?

    Controlled   Satisfied   Rewarded

5. And these words?

    Fortunate   Deprived   Worried

6. And finally, these words?

    Generous   Frugal   Lucky

Have the group leave the piles of coins on the table. Go around the circle and invite people, one by one, to share briefly about an insight they had from this activity.

For the second round of sharing, group members, speaking in any order, can share more deeply in response to the activities from their preparation, focusing on their feelings, stories, and experiences about money (30 minutes). As time allows for the third round, those who wish to may share additional thoughts or reflect on what others have shared (10 minutes).

Closing Activity. Ask your group to brainstorm some easy good deeds that could be done with the coins on the table (i.e., put in the plate at church, scatter on a playground to thrill children, put in a charity coin box). Ask if someone would do one of those things and if others would like to contribute their piles of coins to that cause. Let your group enjoy this exercise without pressure. If no one wants to take responsibility for the coins, tell everyone to take their coin piles home but to be on the lookout for good ways to give them away during the week.

Invite group members to hold hands around the circle and say one or two words about how they are feeling or share an insight they have had at this gathering. Be prepared to go first, and proceed around the circle.

NATURE

Before the Gathering

You'll be bringing a symbol of the element you have chosen to share with the group to the meeting. Read the description of the first round of sharing (see below) and think about your response so that you will be prepared to go first.

At the Gathering

Sharing. For the first round (15 minutes), ask participants to take out their symbol, put it on the table, and describe what element it represents and what draws them to this element. If someone has forgotten to bring something, ask him or her to share what might have been brought. Be prepared to go first to demonstrate. (For example, "I brought a balloon to represent air, because I want to tell a story about something I learned from a bird, but also because I value clarity and lightness.")

For the second round, speaking in any order, group members can share more deeply their feelings about nature, tell a story about an experience they had in nature, or talk about one of the activities or quotations that touched their heart (35 minutes). As time allows in the third round, those who wish to may share additional thoughts or reflect on what others have shared (10 minutes).

Closing Activity. Ask group members, one at a time, to pick up the symbol they brought and say a few words about how it speaks to them of what they have heard and said in the gathering. Be prepared to go first. (For example, "My balloon reminds me that I want to do something about air pollution. I'm going to think about that this week.")

SUCCESS AND FAILURE

Before the Gathering

Read the description of the Closing Activity segment (below). Cut out star shapes about the size of an index card, one for each person. You will find a template for this at the book website, www.HeartToHeartBook.com. Have pens and pencils available for each person. Read the description of the first round of sharing and think about your response so that you will be prepared to go first.

At the Gathering

Sharing. For the first round, ask group members to share briefly about a success or failure in their lives. Be prepared to go first, then proceed around the circle (15 minutes). In the second round, group members, speaking in any order, can share more deeply about success and failure or their experience with one of the activities from their preparation (35 minutes). As time allows in the third round, those who wish to may share additional thoughts or reflect on what others have shared (10 minutes).

Closing Activity. Give each person a paper star. Ask participants to look at the person on their right and think about what that person has shared at this and previous gatherings. Acknowledge that each of us holds our own values and that they show up in the way we live our lives. Ask participants to write on their star one or more values that the person on their right has shown.

Allow time for the group to think about the task and do the writing. When everyone is ready, read your star aloud and give it to the person on your right. Continue around the circle, one at a time.

FRIENDSHIP

Before the Gathering

Obtain or make a simple friendship token of some sort for each person. It may be a personal note, a bookmark, or a piece of candy. Read the description of the first round of sharing (see below) and think about your response so that you will be prepared to go first.

At the Gathering

Sharing. For the first round, ask group members to briefly share something about one of their all-time best friends. This person does not have to be a soul mate, as described in the essay, but should be someone who holds a special place in their heart. Be prepared to share first, then go around the circle (15 minutes). In the second round, speaking in any order, group members can share more deeply their feelings about friendship or their experience with one of the activities from their preparation (35 minutes). As time allows in the third round, those who wish to may share additional thoughts or reflect on what others have shared (10 minutes).

Closing Activity. Say something like, "This is a group of deep sharing. I hope you all feel that we have become friends. I have a little token of friendship for each of you." Pass out the tokens of friendship you have chosen.

Invite group members to hold hands around the circle and say one or two words about how they are feeling or share an insight they have had at this gathering. Be prepared to go first, and proceed around the circle.

DOUBT

Before the Gathering

Put some index cards (two per person) and pens in a basket or other container. Read the description of the Closing Activity segment (below) to familiarize yourself with it. Give some thought to a couple of questions you might use in the ritual. Also read the description of the first round of sharing (see below) and think about your response so that you will be prepared to go first.

At the Gathering

Sharing. For the first round, ask group members to share briefly about a couple of the doubts they are dealing with now (15 minutes). Go first to model the sharing, then continue around the circle. In the second round, people can share more deeply, speaking in any order and focusing on their feelings about doubt or their experience with one of the activities from their preparation (35 minutes). As time allows, in the third round those who wish to may share additional thoughts or reflect on what others have shared (10 minutes).

Closing Activity. Pass the basket around, asking everyone to take a couple of index cards and a pen. Invite group members to write down two unresolved beliefs or issues in their lives in question form. They will be shared anonymously. The questions might be, "What do I believe about God?" or "Do I believe in alternative medicine?" They'll just write the questions; explanations are not necessary.

Give people time to write. Then collect the cards, shuffle them, and put them in the basket. Explain that as you pass the basket around again, each person will draw a card and read it out loud. Note that it doesn't matter if you draw your own card; simply read it like any other. Tell the group that the questions that are deep in our hearts are sacred questions, and they often touch tender areas of our lives. Ask the group to treat these questions with special care, leaving silence between them. Pass the basket to have the cards returned. Invite the group to hold hands and have participants go around the circle saying one or two words about how they are feeling or sharing an insight they have had at this gathering. Be prepared to go first.

MAKING PEACE WITH PARENTS

Before the Gathering

Read the description of the first round of sharing and the Closing Activity segment (below). Think about your responses so that you will be prepared to go first.

At the Gathering

Sharing. For the first round, go around the circle and let people share a brief memory of their parents or parent figures (15 minutes). In the second round, group members, speaking in any order, can share more deeply about memories and feelings related to their parents or parent figures, or they can talk about their experience with the genogram or other activities from their preparation (35 minutes). As time allows in the third round, those who wish to may share additional thoughts or reflect on what others have shared (10 minutes).

Closing Activity. Invite group members into a time of quiet to consider what they have shared about the strengths and weaknesses of their parents or parent figures. Ask them to think of a phrase that describes an ideal inner parent—for example, "My inner parent stays calm in the midst of turmoil" or "My inner parent doesn't take things too seriously." Give them a minute or two to consider this. Go first to model for the group, then proceed around the circle.

After everyone has spoken, invite group members to hold hands around the circle and say one or two words about how they are feeling or share an insight they have had at this gathering. Again, be prepared to go first, and continue around the circle.

SUSTAINABLE LIVING

Before the Gathering

Read the description of the first round of sharing (see below) and think about your response so that you will be prepared to go first.

At the Gathering

Sharing. For the first round (15 minutes), ask group members to share thoughts about their "sustainability diet." Ask: What changes will you consider making for a more sustainable lifestyle? What will sustain you in the process? Go first to model the sharing, then continue around the circle. For the second round, speaking in any order, members can share their feelings, stories, and experiences of how they can affect the future of our world (35 minutes). As time allows for the third round, those who wish to may share additional thoughts or reflect on what others have shared (10 minutes).

Closing Activity. Invite group members to hold hands around the circle and briefly share an insight or feeling about this gathering.
Be prepared to go first, and continue around the circle.

ENDINGS

Before the Gathering

Read the description of the first round of sharing (below) and think about your response so that you will be prepared to go first. Read the description of the Closing Activity segment (below). Fill in the blanks in the following obituary:

This group was born on [date] _____. It was a part of the program of [organization or congregation] _____ _____. The group had [number] _____ members:
[name them, including those who dropped out and when]

_____

_____

_____

_____.

This group met _____ times a month for _____ months. It was a good group. The group's life has now come to an end, and we are gathered here to say our goodbyes to it, to appreciate it for what it was.

At the Gathering

Sharing. In the first round, invite group members to tell about a good goodbye they have experienced in their lifetime. Go first to model the sharing, then continue around the circle (15 minutes). In the second round, speaking in any order, group members can share more deeply, focusing on disengagement, memory, resolution, and blessing in relationship to this group. In particular, if there is something that needs resolution, encourage members to share that (35 minutes). As time allows for the third round, those who wish to may share additional thoughts or reflect on what others have shared (10 minutes).

Closing Activity. Ask participants to form a circle. Tell them that today they are saying goodbye to the group. Acknowledge that the group will be missed and that our lives will be different now that it has ended. However, as the Taoists say, you cannot dip your toe in the same river twice. Invite the group to acknowledge that all life is change, and we can only go forward.

Tell participants that you will have a brief, impromptu memorial service for this group. Explain that, just as in a memorial service for a person, participants will tell the group's story and remember the things about it that they will take into their lives.

Read the obituary that you prepared. Ask who wants to add to it. You might start by saying, "I remember when . . ." Give others a chance to speak. It's all right if this is somewhat lighthearted.

Then say something like, "Now we will have a chance to say our goodbyes to each other. Perhaps we have taken to heart the essay's advice to adopt a goodbye blessing for ourselves." Let this be informal, with each person in the group going to each other person to say goodbye. When this has wound down, get everyone back in a circle.

Closing Words. Comment that the closing reading is a profound blessing and that it holds your hopes for each person in the group.